Accessible Walks in
DORSET

© Marie Houlden, 2015

All Rights Reserved. No part of this publication may be reproduced, stored in a retrieval system, or transmitted in any form or by any means – electronic, mechanical, photocopying, recording, or otherwise – without prior written permission from the publisher or a licence permitting restricted copying issued by the Copyright Licensing Agency, 90 Tottenham Court Road, London W1P 0LA. This book may not be lent, resold, hired out or otherwise disposed of by trade in any form of binding or cover other than that in which it is published, without the prior consent of the publisher.

Moral Rights: The author has asserted her moral right to be identified as the Author of this Work.

Published by Sigma Leisure   an imprint of Sigma Press, Stobart House, Pontyclerc, Penybanc Road, Ammanford, Carmarthenshire SA18 3HP.

British Library Cataloguing in Publication Data
A CIP record for this book is available from the British Library.

ISBN: 978-1-910758-00-7

Typesetting and Design by: Sigma Press, Ammanford.

Cover photograph: Bournemouth Promenade © Marie Houlden

Photographs: © Marie Houlden

Maps: © Sigma Press
Contains OS data © Crown copyright [and database right] 2015

Printed and bound in Great Britain by: TJ International Ltd. Padstow

Disclaimer: the information in this book is given in good faith and is believed to be correct at the time of publication. No responsibility is accepted by either the author or publisher for errors or omissions, or for any loss or injury however caused. Only you can judge your own fitness, competence and experience. Do not rely solely on sketch maps for navigation: we strongly recommend the use of appropriate Ordnance Survey (or equivalent) maps.

Accessible Walks in
DORSET

Marie Houlden

*This book is dedicated to all countryside lovers,
who wish to explore the great outdoors.*

Acknowledgements

I wish to express my thanks and gratitude towards my family, who have not only supported me in writing this book, but who have also taken the time to come and test the routes with me. It was great fun and a fantastic way to spend quality time together!

PREFACE

It was only once I became a mum and a regular pushchair user that I realised just how restricted walking can be due to inaccessible pathways and stiles. Even more importantly, there was simply not enough information available on where you can walk when you have access challenges.

I was determined to produce an entire book for Dorset that gave sensible, accessible walking routes without stiles. I believe you should be able to experience the great outdoors and the fantastic walks that the area has to offer, regardless of your access needs. Walking should be a pleasure, with the focus being on physical exercise, enjoying the fresh air and spending time with your family and friends.

Spotting wildlife along the way is always an added bonus and I have dedicated a small section within each walking description for things to watch out for. My children took great delight in spotting birds or animals that could be added to my *'What to look out for'* sections. We are very lucky as Dorset has many sites that are designated as Sites of Specific Scientific Interest (SSSI) with various rare breeds of national and international importance.

I thoroughly enjoyed exploring the beautiful county of Dorset and it really is a pleasure to be able to share these routes with you. It is my hope that whether you are already a resident in Dorset or a visitor to the area, you will thoroughly enjoy these accessible walks and have as much fun as we did.

Marie Houlden

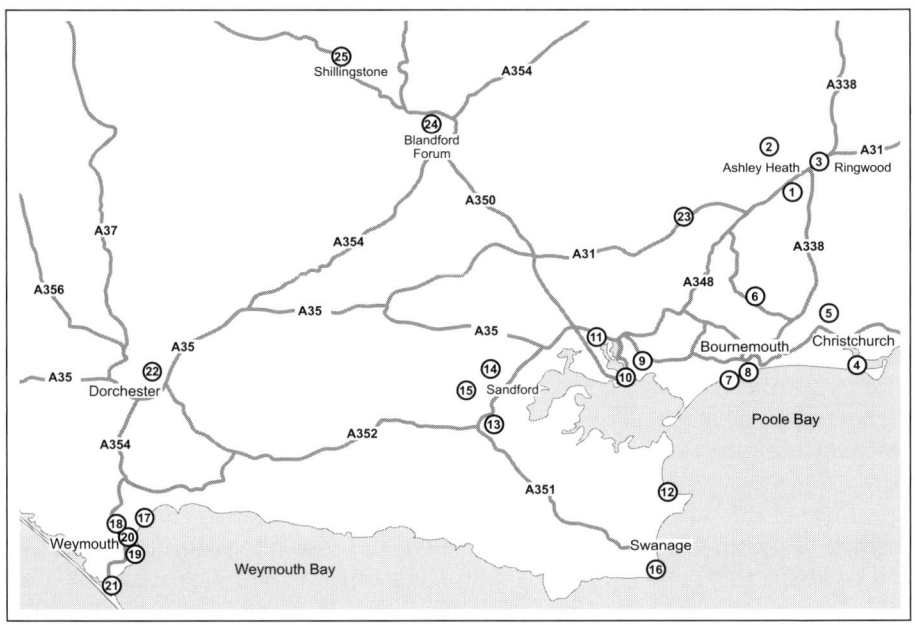

Locations of walks

CONTENTS

Introduction	9
Walk 1: Avon Heath Country Park (Ringwood) Distance: 0.9 miles	11
Walk 2: Moors Valley Country Park (Ringwood) Distance: 2.6 miles	15
Walk 3: Castleman Trail (Ringwood) Distance: 2.9 miles	21
Walk 4: Hengistbury Head (Christchurch) Distance: 3.2 miles	25
Walk 5: St Catherine's Hill (Christchurch) Distance: 2.1 miles *Not suitable for wheelchair users*	30
Walk 6: Stour Valley Nature Reserve (Bournemouth) Distance: 2.4 miles	34
Walk 7: Bournemouth Promenade (Bournemouth) Distance: 4.6 miles	39
Walk 8: Bournemouth Pier to Coy Pond (Bournemouth) Distance: 4.4 miles	44
Walk 9: Poole Park Boating Lake (Poole) Distance: 1.3 miles	49
Walk 10: Poole Quay Trail (Poole) Distance: 3.7 miles	53
Walk 11: Upton Country Park (Poole) Distance: 1.9 miles	58
Walk 12: Old Harry Rocks (Studland/Swanage) Distance: 2.6 miles	63

Walk 13: Wareham Quay – Frome River Walk (Wareham)   68
    Distance: 1.1 miles

Walk 14: Lawsons Clump (Sandford, near Wareham)   72
    Distance: 3.5 miles

Walk 15: Sika Trail (Wareham)   76
    Distance: 4.9 miles
    Not suitable for any wheelchair users

Walk 16: Durlston Country Park (Swanage)   81
    Distance: 1 mile
    Not suitable for wheelchair users

Walk 17: Lodmoor Country Park (Weymouth)   86
    Distance: 1.6 miles

Walk 18: Radipole Nature Reserve (Weymouth)   91
    Distance: 1.7 miles

Walk 19: Nothe Gardens (Weymouth)   95
    Distance: 1.3 miles

Walk 20: Weymouth Harbour Walk (Weymouth)   100
    Distance: 3 miles

Walk 21: The Rodwell Trail (Weymouth)   104
    Distance: 3.8 miles

Walk 22: Dorchester River Walk (Dorchester)   109
    Distance: 2.2 miles

Walk 23: Cannon Hill (Ferndown)   113
    Distance: 2 miles
    Not suitable for wheelchair users

Walk 24: Milldown Nature Reserve (Blandford)   118
    Distance: 0.9 miles

Walk 25: North Dorset Trailway (Shillingstone)   122
    Distance: 6 miles

INTRODUCTION

This book contains twenty-five accessible walks throughout the beautiful county of Dorset. For each walk there is a brief description and then more detailed information about distance, gradient and terrain. From the information provided, you will be able to make an informed decision as to whether the walk suits your particular needs and fitness levels.

I have included walks over a mixture of terrain and within different types of environment, so that there is something for everyone. I have also tried to vary the length of walk, as I appreciate that sometimes a short stroll with a pushchair or wheelchair is all that you want.

There are a few walks that offer not only an enjoyable walk, but also other attractions and things to do in the surrounding area. That way you can complete a shorter walk and still enjoy a proper trip out.

The walks will always give as much information as possible about the history of the area and the wildlife that can be spotted. With young children of my own, I have quickly come to realise how important it is for them to be engaged on our walks. This ensures we all enjoy our time outside and they also benefit from increasing their knowledge.

I always try to make the walk circular, but this is not always possible, particularly when walking around the coast or along disused railway lines. I hope the beauty and tranquillity of some of the linear walks will make up for you having to retrace your steps.

I have always believed that walking should be enjoyable and accessible and to that end none of the walks will have stiles or obstacles that you need to navigate. You can successfully complete the walks in this book whether you choose to walk in a group or alone.

There are full descriptions over the start points, as there is nothing more frustrating than not being able to find the start of the walk. I have chosen to provide postcodes for the start points as experience has taught me that most people rely on satellite navigation (Sat Nav) rather than maps and grid references to reach their destinations.

You will not need an additional Ordnance Survey (OS) map for any of my walking suggestions, as long as you stick to the route described. The walks were completed using a Global Positioning System (GPS) and hence the maps are very accurate and should give you all the detail you need.

Walking research

These walks have been researched with either a standard Maclaren pushchair or the Mountain Buggy all-terrain pushchair. I have ensured that in the walking descriptions I have been as accurate and detailed as possible, allowing you to decide which walks are suitable for you and your own equipment.

I have also considered the needs of those in wheelchairs and noted disabled parking spots and accessible facilities. As the needs and abilities of those in wheelchairs is very diverse, I have left it to the reader to make their own informed decision about whether a route is suitable for them. Where I believe a walk to be totally inappropriate for a wheelchair user, I have clearly stated this on the contents page and within the walk description itself.

Recent years have seen many innovative products becoming available, which have completely transformed walking with a wheelchair. My particular favourite is the FreeWheel attachment (**www.gofreewheel.com**). When added to your standard wheelchair it transforms it into a sturdy all terrain wheelchair, with the capability of navigating even the most challenging of terrains. This product is amazing and as such has really helped to improve the outdoor experience of those with access challenges.

The Dorset County

Dorset is a stunning county situated on the South West coast of England. The county starts near Lyme Regis and extends approximately 87 miles to Christchurch.

Dorset benefits from magnificent coastlines, beautiful country parks, stunning areas of natural beauty and history and wildlife in abundance. These walks will allow you to experience bits of all of these.

As Bournemouth, Poole and Weymouth are all very popular holiday destinations, I have provided a good selection of walks in these areas so that you can spend your time enjoying this beautiful county, rather than wasting your valuable time researching accessible routes.

WALK 1
Avon Heath Country Park

The 600 acres of heath lands are mainly lowland and wet heath, with acid grassland and patches of birch and pine trees. The purple heather that you can see is a beautiful sight in the summer. Work is constantly taking place here, to restore the heath land and provide a valuable environment for the wildlife.

Distance	0.9 miles (1.42km)
Parking	At Avon Heath Country Park (charges apply). There are four disabled parking spaces. Gates open at 8am and close at 6.30pm or dusk, whichever comes first. As you head from Ringwood to St Leonards on the A31, take the road called Brocks Pine which is the first turning off of the roundabout, directly opposite the road to St Leonards and a Little Chef, this will take you straight to the country park. The postcode for sat nav users, is BH24 2DA, however this covers a wide area, so it is best to follow the brown tourist signs once you are close by
Facilities	Toilets (the baby change facility is a table in the ladies toilet and there is a designated disabled toilet, which is open all the time), café, discovery centre, children's play area and telephone box. There are plenty of bins, dog bins and benches throughout the park
Gradient	Mostly flat, with a couple of undulating sections
Terrain	Mainly gravel, with some sections of woodland terrain, i.e. fallen leaves, twigs, bark and sand. It is worth bearing in mind that it might be a bit bumpy in places
Map	OS Explorer OL22

The Area
Avon Heath Country Park is managed and maintained by Dorset Countryside. They do not charge for entry, but car parking charges do apply throughout the year.

There is so much wildlife to see here and as such the park is classified as a site of specific scientific interest. Interestingly, the park is home to some rare wildlife, such as the Dartford Warbler and the Nightjar and therefore has international importance.

The Walk
The track you will be following through the park is very wide and great if you are walking with other people and wish to chat. It is also ideal for toddlers or younger children who want to walk and run ahead independently, as the route is entirely through heath land and away from any traffic. As dogs are allowed off the lead in this area, you may need to watch for any occasional mess that has not been cleared up by responsible owners.

Starting from the visitor centre turn left and follow the gravel path towards the gate which will take you through to the heath land. You will need to go through the wide gate.

Path at Avon Heath Country Park

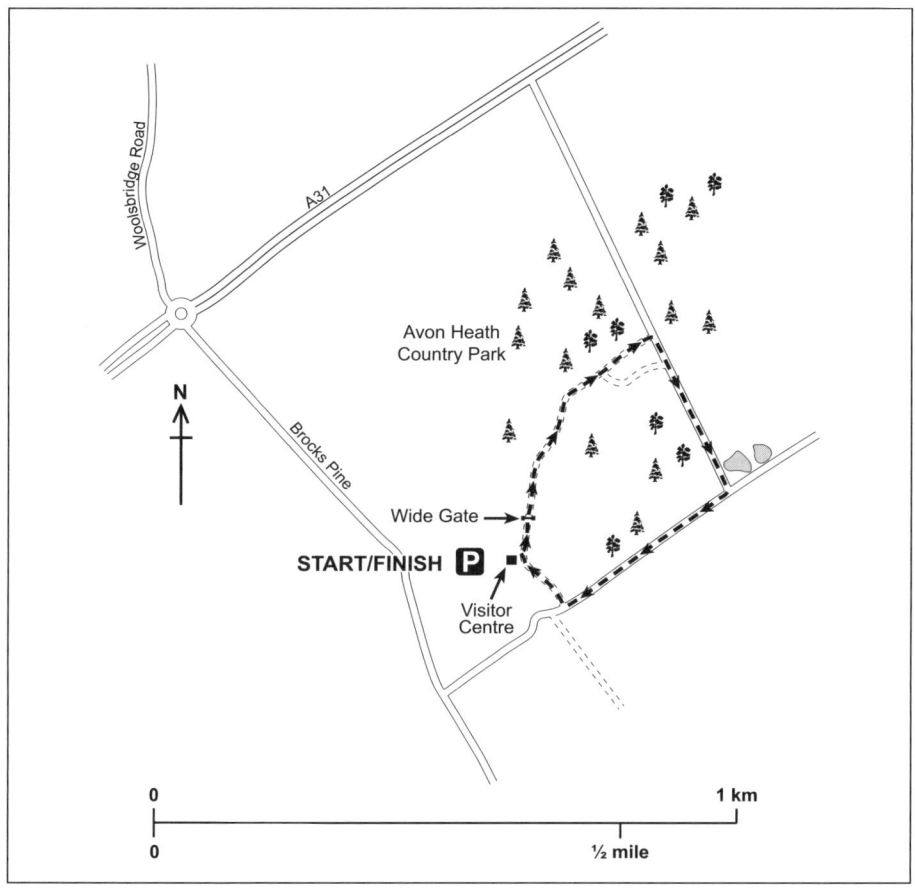

You will see a path that veers off to the left, but you need to remain on the main path. As you continue on the route, be aware of tree roots coming through the ground in a couple of places.

The path will then change from gravel to more of a woodland terrain, it is still very easy to walk over, you will come to a T junction in the trees and you need to head right.

You will now be walking on a path that is tree lined and very wide. This part of the route is a great place for children to run ahead and explore as you will still be able to see them.

The path then goes back to being gravel with a few undulating patches. You will notice a pond to the left, which is completely fenced off, but great for spotting some wildlife.

At the next T junction there will be a cattle grid and gate to the left and you need to stay on the main path and head right. You will come across another track that veers off to the left, but again you need to remain on the main path and walk towards the next cattle grid. Go through the gate and you will now be able to see the visitor centre ahead of you and the starting point of your walk.

What to see and do
There is a fantastic play park by the visitor centre and café. They have recently renovated this area and they now benefit from having pieces of equipment and sculptures that have been made from wood. There is also a children's favourite - the zip wire!

There is plenty of space on the green behind the café to have a picnic and play ball games. You can also hire out the stationary Bar B Q's.

The Heathland Discovery Centre has some interesting and interactive displays for children and the indoor viewing hide is very popular for getting a closer look at the wildlife.

What to look out for
This is a truly fantastic place to spot wildlife and is a great educational site for children and adults alike. You will see Emperor Dragonflies, bird boxes with a variety of birds popping in and out of them, rabbits, squirrels and a huge variety of heather scrubs and trees. If you are really lucky you may even catch sight of a buzzard as he soars over the heath land looking for food.

WALK 2
Moors Valley Country Park

Moors Valley is an extremely popular place for those wishing to have a family day out. From the visitor centre to the adventure park, there really is something here for everyone.

The walk has exceptionally easy access for pushchair and wheelchair users and as such this is a lovely and relaxing walk, with an abundance of wildlife to take in and enjoy.

The adventure playground at Moors Valley Country Park

Distance	2.6 miles (4.12 km)
Parking	There is plenty of parking available in the park, charges do apply, however there is no entrance fee for the park itself. There are 13 disabled spaces, which can be found right by the visitor centre. As you travel down the dual carriageway from Bournemouth on the A338 and reach the Ashley Heath roundabout, take the road straight ahead of you, which is sign posted to Three Legged Cross. There will also be brown tourist signs for the park from this point. Continue on this road until you have gone through the village of Ashley Heath and you will see the entrance to Moors Valley Country Park on the right hand side. The postcode for the park is BH24 2ET, however this covers a wide area and once you have reached Three Legged Cross, it would be better to follow the directions above and the brown tourist signs
Facilities	Café, toilets (Baby change and family cubicles. There are also plenty of accessible toilets throughout the park, with the newly refurbished toilets at the visitor centre also including a tracking hoist system) visitor centre, children's adventure park, miniature railway, benches, bins, dog bins. The park is open from 8am till dusk or 8pm each day. A wheelchair or scooter can be borrowed from the visitor centre, but it would be a good idea to book in advance - 01425 470721
Gradient	Flat with a couple of very short inclines and declines
Terrain	Mainly tarmac, there are a few sections of mesh covered wooded boardwalks and several concrete bridges to cross
Map	OS Explorer OL22

The Area

This amazing country park is situated ten miles from Bournemouth and on the edge of the New Forest National Park, one of the few places in England where the landscape has remained unchanged over the years.

This particular path through Moors Valley is very peaceful and tranquil in places, particularly when you are away from the main hub of activities.

The wildlife and foliage is amazing and the colours in autumn as the trees are shedding their leaves are simply stunning. This walk has many viewpoints, benches and information boards where you can stop to appreciate the beauty of the area and the wildlife it has to offer. It truly is a magnificent place to walk around and explore.

The Walk

The walk starts by the visitor centre, so with this on your right, walk past the visitor centre, the coffee snack bar and toilets and then go over the zebra crossing. In front of you will be the children's adventure play ground and to your left a dog park.

The tarmac path veers around to the right and then goes down a slight decline. Follow this path around to the right and in front of you will be the miniature railway station. Keep on this path and you will past the station on your right and you will now be walking along the lakeside. The picnic area to your left is a great place to enjoy the views and let children play.

As you continue on this path you will pass a decking area on your right with a large dragonfly sculpture, this is a great place to spot resident dragonflies and fish. Along this section of the path there are several places where you will see allocated fishing pitches for people trying to catch a fish or two and also for the rangers holding educational workshops.

Walk past the gravel track on your left and as you continue on this path you will see the miniature train depot on the other side of the lake. You will come to a bridge with a concrete floor and you need to cross over this and then take a left, going over the wooden bridge. The signpost will say ' Nature Trail' and 'Potterne Wood'.

As you cross the bridge you will very quickly come to a T Junction and you will need to go right. Follow the path all the way to the tip of the golf course. You will see a wooden fence to your left and a pathway that takes you onto the golf course. Keep walking on the main path, walking over the bridge and then take the path straight on that is sign posted to the 'Crane Lake and Forest'. You will go down a small decline and you will need to take the path immediately on the left. You will now have the golf course on your right and a small stream to your left.

You will soon come to a turning on your left signed posted 'Crane Lake and

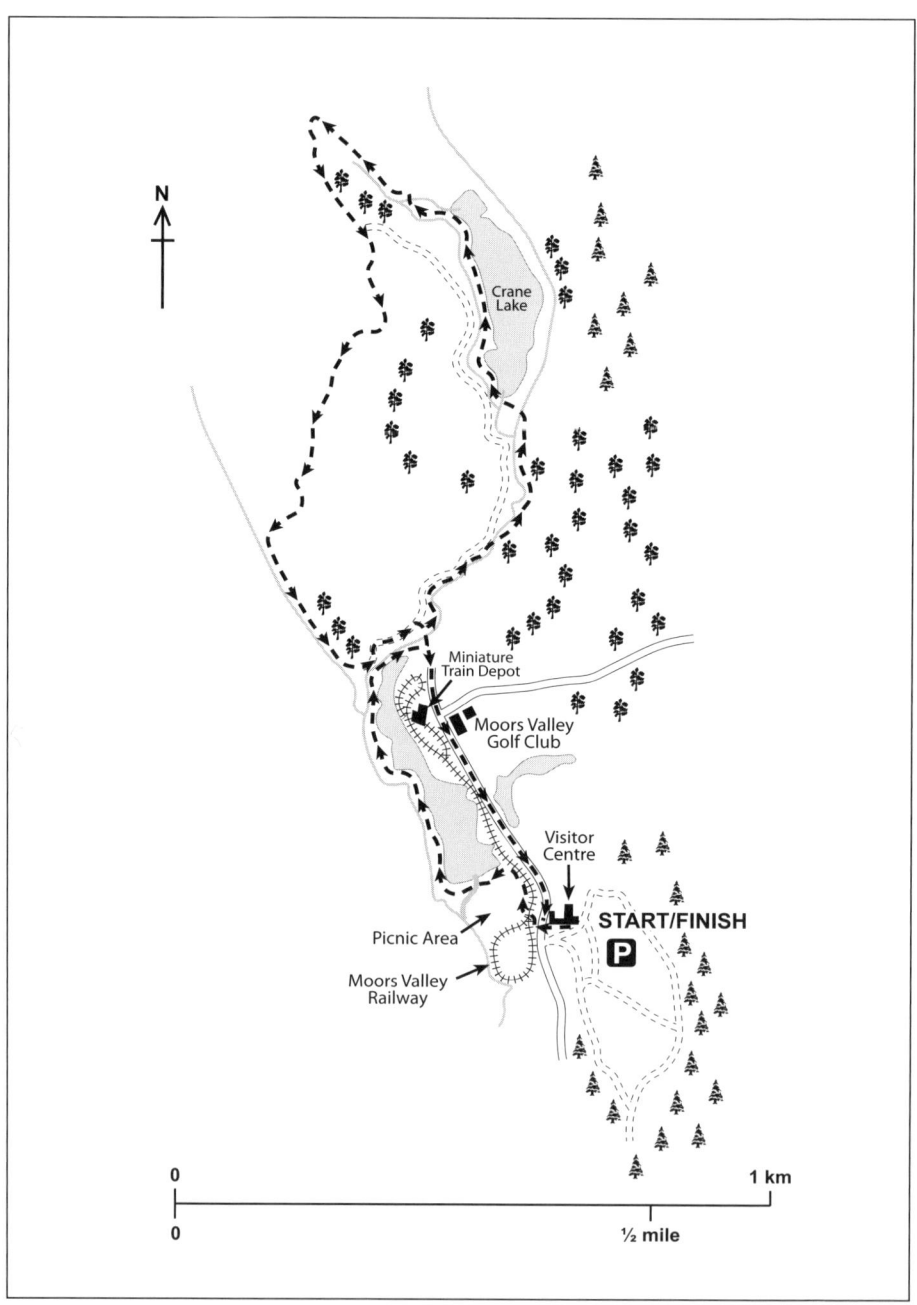

Potterne Wood' and you will see a small wooden bridge. You need to walk over the bridge and keep on the tarmac track. To your right will be the lake and an information board about the variety of birds you can see.

Once you have taken the time to enjoy the views of the lake and spotted some of the birds, continue on this track as it meanders around the lake. Stay on this path and you will pass over another bridge. When you come to a T Junction you will need to go left which is signed posted 'Visitor Centre and Railway'. After crossing the bridge you will need to go left again.

As you continue on this tarmac path with the golf course on either side of you, you will walk past a couple of gravel tracks that take you onto the golf course. Eventually you will come to a wooden boardwalk, covered with wire mesh – take care here as it can be slippery. You will then walk along another section of tarmac pathway before coming to a second wooden boardwalk. The path will then revert back to tarmac. You will take the pathway to the right going back over the wooden bridge, which started this section of the walk.

From here go straight on towards the train depot, this will then be on your right. There are a variety of facilities here that you can make use of and you can even ride the train back to the start of the walk.

Walking past the train depot join the tarmac path between the road and the railway and walk straight on towards the miniature railway station at the start of the walk. You can either choose to walk alongside the railway track or join the road back to the visitor centre.

What to see and do
As the majority of this walk is on tarmac, it is an ideal place for older children to cycle or scoot. It is also a very safe environment and sturdy terrain for toddlers who want to try and walk some of the route.

The adventure playground is an ideal place for children to burn off some additional energy before heading home.

Trandems are available to hire from the cycle hire centre and provide an excellent way to enjoy the park.

What to look out for
There are so many wonderful birds living at Moors Valley and if you are lucky you will get to see moorhens, mallards, swans, coots and also some of the harder to spot birds, such as kingfishers, herons, Tawny owls and cormorants.

Along the route look out for the bird boxes hidden in the trees, especially by the lake.

We were able to spot some amazing bright red and white toadstools (Fly Agaric), along the route, however they are highly poisonous so please do take care with children and dogs.

WALK 3
Castleman Trail – Ringwood to Ashley Heath

The Castleman Trail covers 16.5 miles in total and is part of a disused railway line that used to run from Southampton to Dorchester. It is named after a Wimborne solicitor called Charles Castleman who was chiefly responsible for getting the original railway built in the 1840s. It was open to the public in June 1847 and due to various plans to make the railway system more viable the line was closed to passengers shortly after 1964.

Due to the stunning scenery and wide paths along the trail, this route is very popular with ramblers, dog walkers and cyclists. The path is very wide and ideal if you have a double buggy. At the start of the trail you will have to go through a metal structure, which is used to stop motocross bikes speeding along the trail and causing a nuisance and danger to others. This may cause an access issue for some wheelchair users.

Distance	2.90 miles (5.80 km)
Parking	Free parking in Hurn Lane for approximately 20 cars, although there are no allocated disabled spots. As you head on the B3081 from Verwood and turn into Hurn Lane, the car park is immediately on the left. The car park surface is gravel and puddles are very common when it has been raining
Facilities	Dog bins, shop. There are no toilets on this walk
Gradient	Flat
Terrain	Tarmac, gravel, woodland
Map	OS Explorer OL22

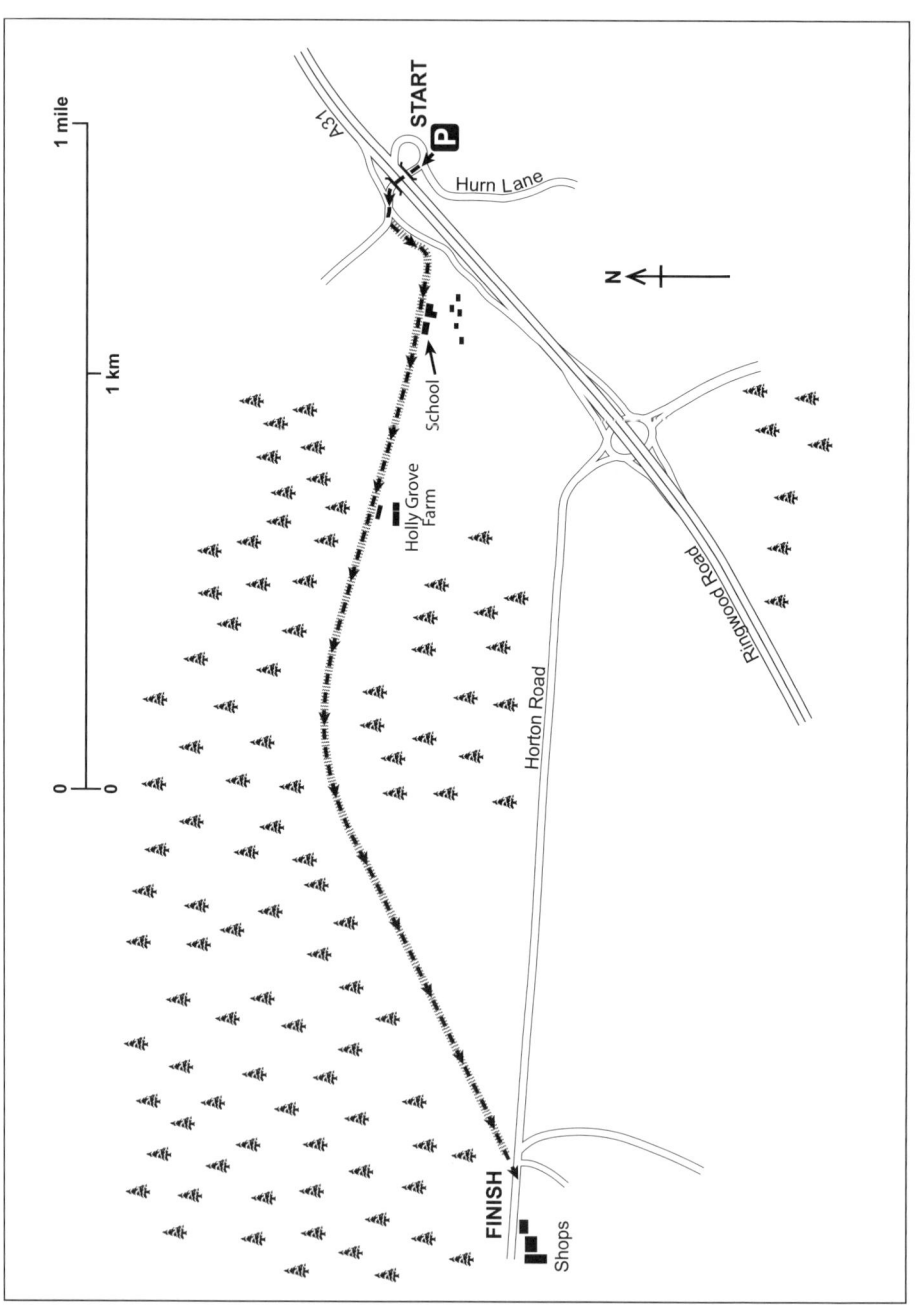

The Area

The area around Ringwood to Ashley Heath is very peaceful and tranquil. It is right on the edge of the New Forest National Park and as such the landscape is very unspoilt.

For most of the walk you will have building and houses on your left hand side and the woodland and various meadows and fields on the right. Although you can initially hear the busy road, it is not long before the walk becomes much more tranquil and the only noise you hear will be from birds singing in the treetops.

Its is worth noting that the trail can get a bit muddy when it is wet and so the path would become more challenging for wheelchair users.

The Walk

Starting from the car park cross over Hurn Lane and walk on the pavement towards and then under the bridge. You will then need to cross two more roads, which are situated very close together. After crossing the second road, you will see the start of the walk to your left and a green and yellow sign saying 'Castleman Trail' pointing towards 'Ashley Heath'.

Part of the Castleman Trail

As you start out on this path, you will initially pass by houses, a school and various buildings on the left and to your right there will be fields and meadows, woodlands and a quiet country lane.

Eventually you will see a grey concrete building on the left which is part of an industrial complex and immediately after this and directly in front of you will be part of the quiet lane, leading into the complex. Cross the road rejoining the gravel path and continue straight on.

After some time you will pass a wooden bridge on the left, just in front of a row of houses. Continue straight on and eventually walk past a signpost on the right directing you to West Moors and the main road. Many people will go to Moors Valley Country Park by taking the turning signposted to your right.

Eventually you will come to the end of this section of the Castleman trail and you will see in front of you the main road, traffic lights and a shop where you can get refreshments before turning around and retracing your steps.

What to see and do
We spotted various birds flying overhead and in the trees. There were a few squirrels, however as soon as they saw our dog they quickly scampered up the nearest tree!

This trail is an excellent place for children to gain their confidence for cycling on gravel and woodland terrains. Older children can also run ahead and explore and still remain in your sight.

What to look out for
Along side the trail there are several long stretches that have a deep trench between the trail and the houses, these can get filled with water and are a favourite with dogs!

WALK 4
Hengistbury Head

This is a breathtaking walk around a beautiful headland between Christchurch and Bournemouth. There are a variety of habits, wildlife and rare plant species here and as such it makes a great educational resource. Due to its diversity of wildlife and geology it has been designated as a Site of Specific Scientific Interest, with significant archaeological importance and interest.

With beautiful views and such educational importance, this stunning headland attracts over one million visitors a year.

Distance	Approx 3.2 miles (5 km). There is the option to take in the beach and this additional path is about 400 metres long
Parking	There is a pay and display car park very close to the Café and toilets. There are five designated disabled spaces. The Sat Nav postcode for the Hiker Café is BH6 4EN. Follow the B3059 from Bournemouth into Southbourne, turn right into Marine Road and then left onto Southbourne Overcliffe Drive. At the mini roundabout go straight over on the Southbourne Coast Road. At the end of this road turn right, you will pass a golf course on your left and the car park will be on your right
Facilities	Accessible toilets with baby change (you need to get a key from the café), Hiker Café and Mudeford café, ice-cream bars and land train. There are also plenty of benches, bins and dog bins on the route
Gradient	Mostly flat - a few inclines in places

Terrain	Mainly tarmac and then sand at Mudeford. If you want to go onto the beach at Mudeford, you will have to navigate quite a bit of sand. The all terrain pushchair coped very well with this, but I would not recommend trying this with a wheelchair, unless you are confident it can cope with it. There is also an additional route of gravel and sand, if you to experience some of the amazing views of the beach facing out towards the English Channel
Map	OS Explorer OL22

The Area

Hengistsbury head is a truly magical place to explore, no doubt as the headland is seeped in history and clearly has some interesting stories to tell. It is believed that the area played an important role in national trade and defence many years ago and was in fact an Iron Age trading centre.

When the wind is blowing the view of the waves is truly spectacular and I would strongly recommend taking in the additional trail.

The paths here are for the most part traffic free and hence a great place children to run ahead and explore. The path is also very popular with cyclists, dog owners and other keen ramblers.

The Walk

Starting from the pay and display car park walk towards the Hiker Café and the adjoining toilet block. The walk starts from the front of the café, by the land train station. With your back to the café walk on the wide tarmac path, heading towards the building situated on the right hand side of the path.

Please do be aware that the land train runs throughout the day and on your walk you will probably see the train at least once or twice. Although cars are not generally allowed on this track, you can sometimes see maintenance vehicles driving up to the huts at Mudeford, and at certain times of the year hut owners are granted permission to use the track to clear out their possessions.

Continue past the building and you will see a path on the right that leads you to the cliffs and the ocean. This is the additional part of the walk, which can be done at either the start or end of the walk. When the wind is blowing in from the Atlantic Ocean, the waves look magnificent crashing on the beach and it is quite a breathtaking sight.

For now, you will be continuing on towards Mudeford and the bay overlooking Christchurch and Mudeford will be to your left. This is a very popular spot for dog walkers and you can often see dogs swimming in the water.

As you continue forward on this tarmac path, you will see that the walk goes through a wooded and shaded area. Just before the wooded area you will see a Bird Sanctuary on the right. Keep on the main path and you will then come to the Mudeford Sandpit Lagoon on the left, this is a great place to stop and look for birds. Across the lagoon you will also be able to see an array of colourful beach huts.

The path will now begin to veer around to the left and the terrain becomes more sandy. You will pass beach huts and a toilet block on your right. Along this path there are a variety of small tracks that lead you to the beach,

Beach huts at Mudeford

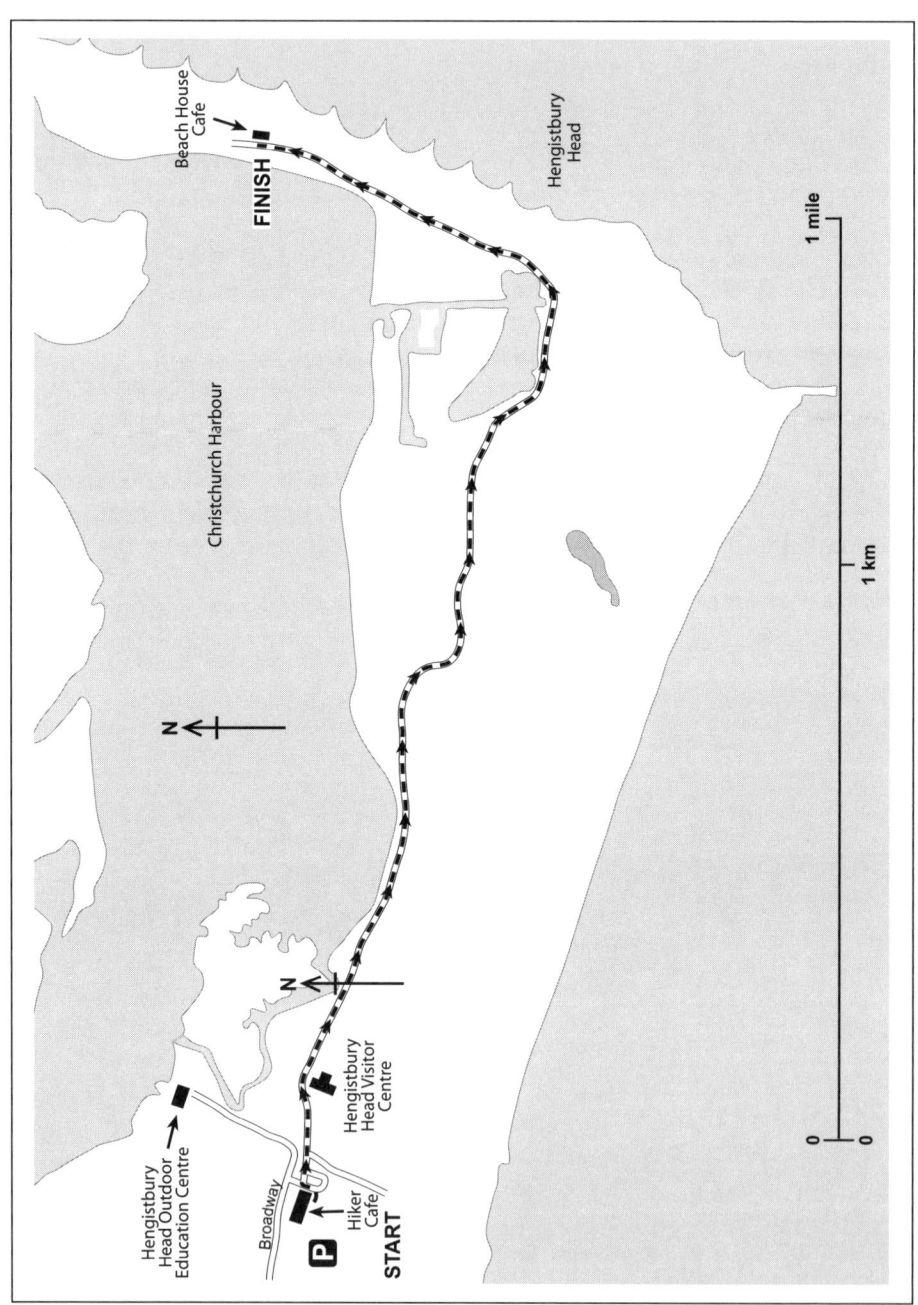

however the main path to the beach is by the café at the end of this walk. Continue on this path and walk past the land train station on the left and head towards the café, which is situated on the right.

This is the end of the walk and you now need to turn around and retrace your steps. You always have the option of taking the land train back to the Hiker Café and they are very happy to carry pushchairs and dogs!

What to see and do

There is a boat ride that can be done around the Bay of Mudeford.

Children will enjoy the beach at Mudeford, where they can play happily in the sand or paddle in the sea.

The open green spaces by the car park at the start of the walk, is a very popular spot for kite flying.

What to look out for

There are always plenty of boats and yachts to spot either out in the bay or moored up in Mudeford Quay.

There are many varied and beautiful birds to see on this walk. We were able to spot gulls, mallards, spotted redshanks and wigeons, although these are just a few of the types of birds that can be seen here.

By the building close to the Hiker Café, you can often see chickens running loose and there are regularly cattle in the fields.

WALK 5
St Catherine's Hill

This is one of the most challenging walks in the book due to the gradual incline from the car park to the start of St Catherine's Hill and then the short steep section to reach the top of the hill. As long as you are fit and prepared for the steep hill, it really is worth the effort, as the views over the Avon Valley and towards the Isle of Wight are fantastic. This is not a walk I would recommend for wheelchair users.

Distance	2.1 miles (3.36 km)
Parking	There is a small car park at the bottom of St Catherine's Hill Lane/Marsh Lane in Christchurch. There are no parking charges. The postcode for St Catherine's Hill Lane is BH23 2NL, this covers the entire lane and the car park is at the very start of the lane, just off from the main B3070 Fairmile road
Facilities	Dog bins and a few benches
Gradient	Undulating and very steep in once section. As mentioned above, not suitable for wheelchair users
Terrain	Gravel, small compacted stone woodland and sand – tree roots in places
Map	OS Explorer OL22

The Area
Situated in the north of Christchurch, St Catherine's Hill covers an area of 35 hectares, which is mainly heathland and coniferous trees. It is home to a variety of wildlife and therefore various bodies work together to ensure nature preservation.

In the distant past, St Catherine's Hill was used as a look out and more recently as a military training ground, particularly for both World Wars.

The tranquil and relaxing atmosphere here today is wonderful and the aroma of pine trees is intoxicating - the Victorians were certainly right with their belief that pine trees can benefit those returning to health.

The Walk

With your back to the entrance to the car park you will see an information board to your left next to a small track. You need to take the main wider lane slightly to the right, which will take you towards the houses situated in St Catherine's Hill Lane.

Keep on this track and head straight up the hill. You will see a track to the right that leads to more houses and then another smaller track on the left, but you need to continue on.

You will then come to a wooden gate and an information board, these can be found next to the entrance to the Christchurch Gun Club. For your information when the red flag is flying, shooting is taking place. You can still complete the walk in safety; just don't be surprised to hear gunshots coming from their compound.

You will now take the woodland path to the left of the notice board and this will take you up a steep hill. This is the toughest part of the walk, however the views at the top more than make up for the effort exerted.

At the top of the hill you will see a viewpoint to your right and you need to take the path to the left. The path will shortly fork and you will be taking the path to the left. You will see a metal fence and this is the

Path at St Catherine's Hill

31

boundary of the Christchurch Gun Club, if you look through the mesh wire you can see their facilities. The path to the right simply leads to more viewpoints over the valley, however there is no accessible path here.

You will now be staying on this main wide path until you come to a rest area and information board. On the way to the rest area you will pass two large white concrete buildings on your left, which are reservoirs for the area. The path is very easy to navigate and as the trees are sparsely planted, children and dogs can run around and explore without being out of your sight.

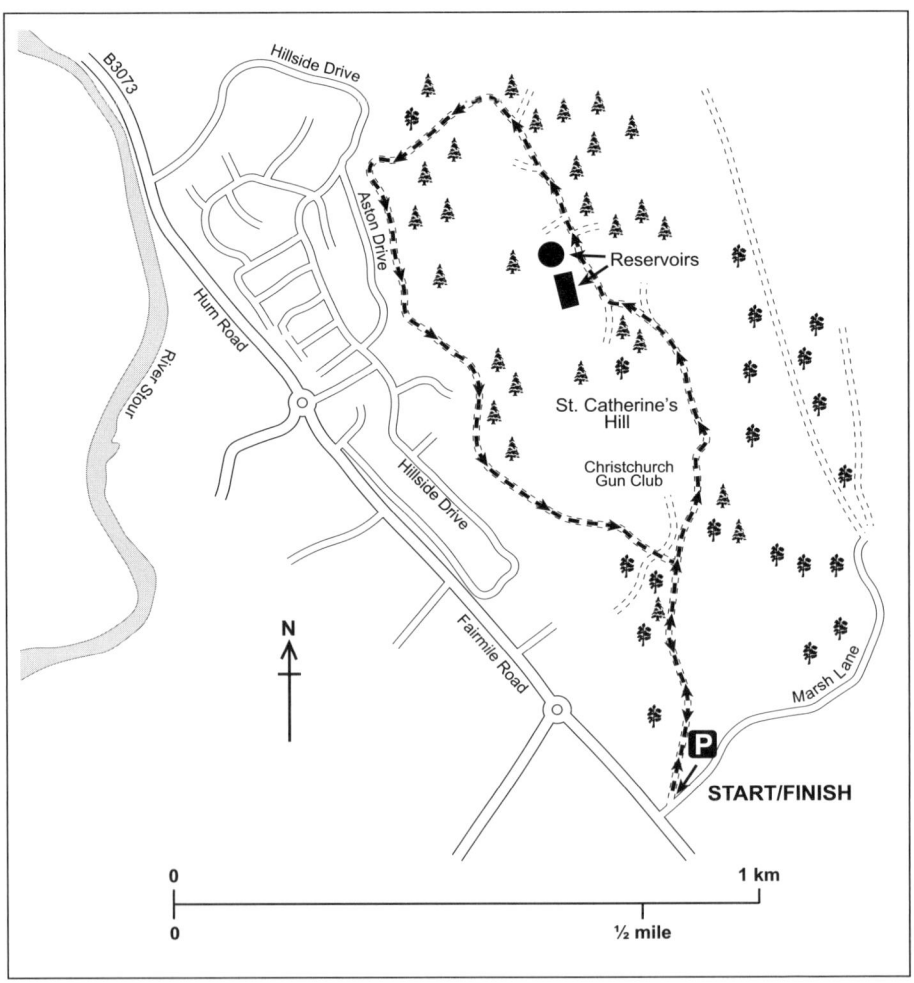

Approximately 200 metres from the rest area you will come across a turning to the left, which you will need to take. The path takes you downhill and you will see an obvious track down through the trees. If you keep heading straight you will join another main path that backs onto a residential area and is the edge of the woodland.

Take the path to the left, passing the exit to the woodland and keep straight on. As you walk on this path you will have houses to your right and the woodland to your left. You will pass two further exits to the park, which lead down to residential areas. You need to keep following the meandering path around the edge of the woodland.

You will eventually come to a point in the walk where you could go straight on or head to the right. Go straight on here for approximately 50 metres, as this will then take you to another lane, which leads to the Christchurch Gun Club. It is worth noting that the lane is quite concealed if cars are not driving past, as it simply looks like more woodland.

Once you reach the lane turn left and head back up towards the Christchurch Gun Club, you will see the entrance to St Catherine's Hill in front of you and you should recognise the track that you first walked up, to your right. Head down the track back to the car park.

What to see and do
The views across the Avon Valley are truly breathtaking. If it is a clear day you will even be able to see over to the Isle of Wight.

What to look out for
In autumn you will see squirrels all over the woodland floor collecting food before hibernating.

If you look very closely you may catch sight of sand lizards, adders and smooth snakes.

The woodland also has an abundance of birds living in the trees. Common to the area are birds such as the Dartford Warbler and the Nightjar.

WALK 6

Stour Valley Nature Reserve (Bournemouth)

The River Stour is approximately 64 miles long and this accessible two mile stretch of nature reserve, alongside the river is a great place to explore the vast amount of wildlife living in the rivers, meadows and hedgerows.

Bournemouth has a number of nature reserves, however in 2007 this was the first one to receive a Green Flag award, which proudly it still holds.

Distance	2.4 miles (4.02 km)
Parking	There is free parking and two designated disabled parking spaces. As you travel along the A3060 (Castle Lane West in Bournemouth) turn at the traffic lights into Muscliffe Lane and then take the second turning on your left, which is Granby Road. There is a car park immediately on the right
Facilities	Car parking, benches and dog bins
Gradient	Mainly flat with a couple of undulating sections
Terrain	Gravel, a section of compacted stone and few sections of wooded boardwalks, which are very smooth and easy to navigate. I would only undertake this walk in a wheelchair/tramper that is all terrain and very sturdy
Map	OS Explorer OL22

The Area

Stour Valley is a nature reserve situated in the north part of Bournemouth, it is home to 400 plant species and approximately 50 types of birds.

For the majority of the walk the path is gravel and very sturdy underfoot. When the leaves fall this can be a bit slippery and muddy in places. If there has been heavy rainfall you can expect to see puddles along the way, however they do provide excellent entertainment for children who want to splash about in them. The path is also a good width, which is ideal for double pushchairs and wider wheelchairs or trampers.

The area is highly popular with dog walkers and every time we have walked here, we have always found it to be very social. The dogs here always look like they are having such a great time and my children love seeing the dogs play. Even though you are walking along the river you will not go too far without passing another walker, fisherman or dog owner.

The Walk

Starting from the car park and with your back to the Muscliffe Lane, head towards the lane on the left. Effectively you will go out of the car park entrance and onto the pavement for a short distance, before turning right into a lane. Go through the gate and walk past the building on your right hand side. This track then becomes gravel and meanders down to the river.

You will pass some steps and a slope on your right, which is an alternative route from and back to the car park. In the car park you will see the path directly behind the notice board, you will however need to navigate a short slope. I tried this with my all-terrain pushchair and found this to be very accessible, however I would be inclined to stick to the slightly longer route if in a wheelchair.

Once you reach the river edge, you will take the path to the left, which is signposted to 'Dudsbury'.

You will soon walk along a section of the walk with a small wooden fence either side of the path. It is worth noting that the majority of the walk is not fenced in, so care should be taken with excited young children who are keen to explore.

Go over the wooden boardwalk and shortly you will see that the path widens out and you will now have meadows and fields to your left. You will then arrive at the second fishing platform where children can get closer to the waters edge to spot fish and other river wildlife.

As you continue on this path you will walk past several meadows and fields,

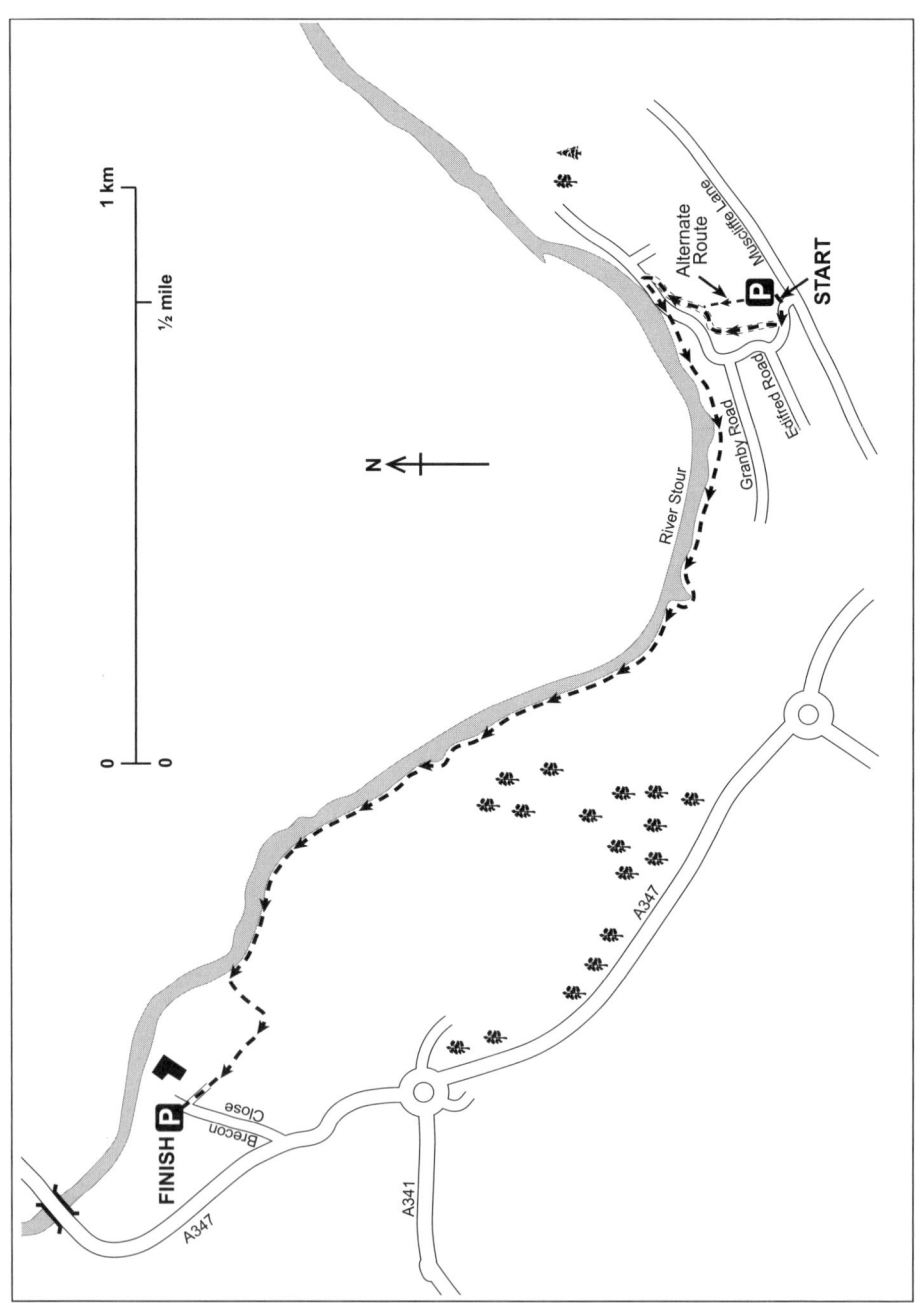

all separated by hedgerows filled with wildlife. You will then come to a patch of the walk that is compacted stone and this will veer to the right before taking you over a weir.

You will eventually come to part of the path that then heads to the left, with a signpost that says 'Brecon Close Car Park'. As you walk through the trees and around the bend you will see an information board and houses in front of you. You have now reached the end of the walk and you will need to turn around and retrace your steps.

What to see and do
There are various spots along the riverside where we saw fisherman trying their hand at catching fish. There are also two very distinct fishing platforms, one at the start of the walk and the other about halfway along, which is ideal for children to get really close to the water and spot fish. You will often see dogs here, using the slopes as an easy way to get in and out of the river.

What to look out for
If you are really lucky you may be able to see one of the resident herons

Path at Stour River Walk

swooping down to catch a fish – this was certainly a highlight for us! There are also plenty of gulls, magpies and swans. The Stour Valley is also home to roe deer, otters, kingfishers, buzzards and kestrels, although these are much harder to spot.

In the fields and meadows on the opposite side of the river we were able to see horses and cows.

WALK 7
Bournemouth Promenade (West Undercliff)

This is an easy and stunning walk along the tarmac promenade from Bournemouth to Sand Banks, with views all around Poole Bay. The walk is linear and hence you can make the walk as long or as short as you like. With the Bournemouth Pier so close you could extend your walk and take in some additional accessible attractions.

Distance	4.6 miles (7.52 km)
Parking	There is a pay and display car park by the Durley Chine Harvester with plenty of spaces and great access to the promenade. There are 7 designated disabled parking spaces. The Sat Nav postcode for the Durley Chine is BH2 5JG and the car park is right next to it. As you turn into West Overcliff Drive, you will then need to turn immediately left into the road that will take you down to West Undercliff Promenade
Facilities	Various toilet blocks along the promenade, most of these are accessible with a RADAR key, which can be collected from the nearest beach office. Pub, restaurants (Harvester has a ramp and an accessible toilet), cafés and snack/ice –cream bars, bins, dog bins, benches
Gradient	Flat
Terrain	Tarmac
Map	OS Explorer OL15 and OL22

39

The Area
Bournemouth is situated right on the south coast of England and it is a hugely popular town to live in and to visit. It has seven miles of golden sands and as such the promenade is a popular place for walkers and runners, cyclists, dog owners, skaters and those who use wheelchairs. The views of Poole Bay are truly breathtaking and on a clear day you can see all the way to the Isle of Wight. As the terrain is entirely tarmac, the walk can be completed regardless of the weather and is accessible to everyone. The various pubs, cafes and restaurants available, will always provide a welcome rest and refreshment stop.

The Walk
Starting from the car park by West Undercliff Promenade, walk down towards the beach front with the Harvester public house and restaurant on your left.

When you reach the promenade you will be able to see the Bournemouth Pier to your left and the sea directly in front of you. Turn right and start your walk along the West Undercliff Promenade, this fantastic path will take you around Poole Bay, passing Alum Chine, Branksome Chine and Candford Cliffs Chine before arriving at the notorious Sand Banks resort. This is reported to be the fourth most expensive place in the world to live and is home to many famous individuals.

Along your route, you will pass several road and path turnings to your right which take you to the cliff top, other car parks and wooded areas or gardens, including the Branksome Chine Nature Reserve. This consists of 13 acres of steep sided wooded valleys and ridges, as this is not accessible I would recommend you keep walking until you reach Sandbanks.

When you reach the end of the tarmac walk way at Sandbanks, you can either stop and enjoy some refreshments or turn around and retrace your steps.

What to see and do
There will always be plenty of nice spots on the beach to stop and build a sand castle. You may even see a surfer or two in the water!

You will see lots of brightly coloured beach huts on this walk. There is even the opportunity to rent one if you fancied a full day at the beach. Bournemouth are proud to offer fully accessible beach huts that have internal space for up to four wheelchairs.

If you decide to explore the promenade towards Bournemouth Pier you will

Bournemouth promenade

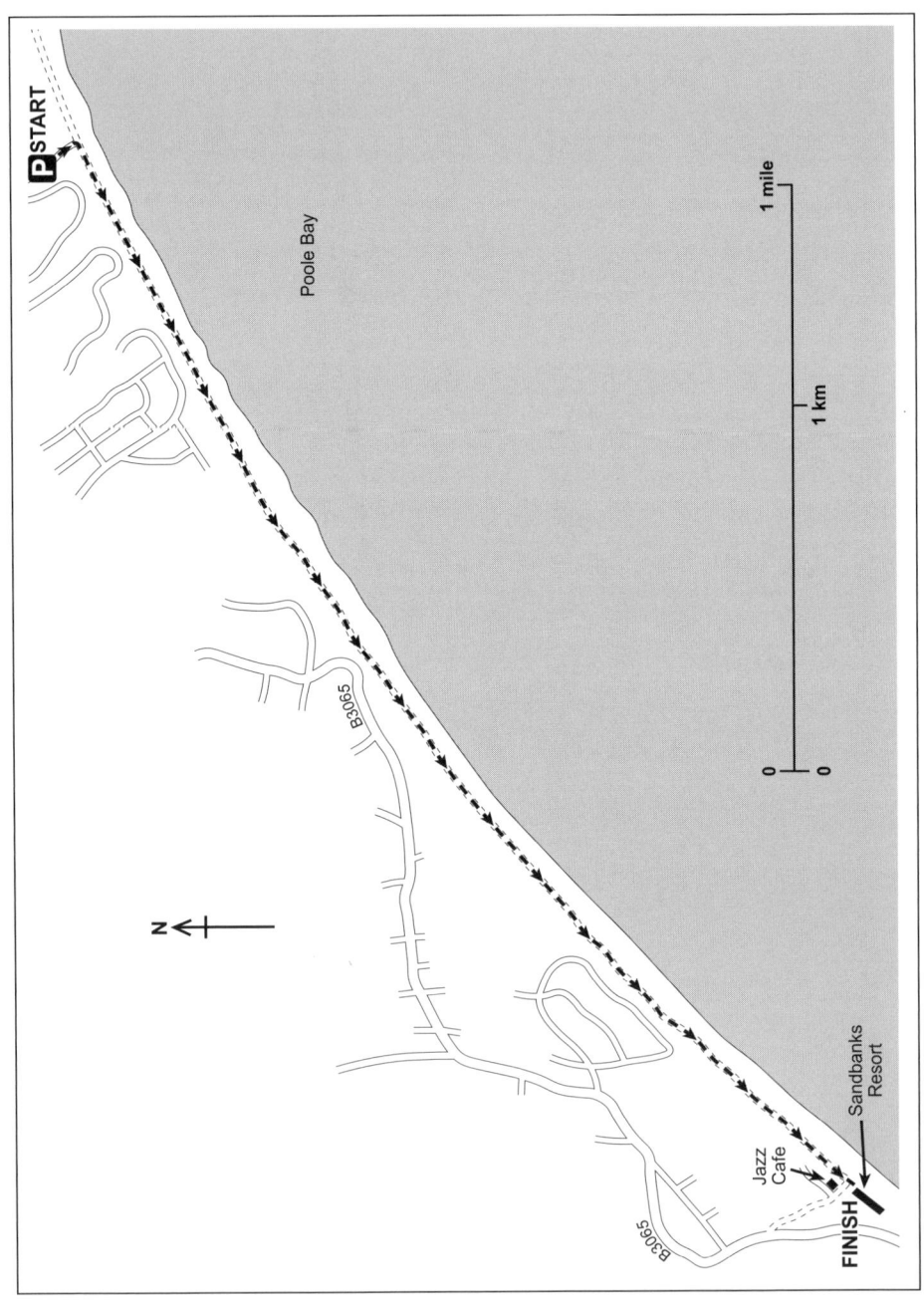

find plenty of things to keep children entertained – the aquarium, amusement arcades, fairground rides and the pier itself. There is also an abundance of cafes and restaurants to try. If after all this exploring the children, (or you!) are too tired to walk back to the car, you could hop on the land train which takes you back to the Durley Chine Harvester. Permanent wheelchair users, plus one carer can travel for free on the land train.

Why not rent out one of the beach going wheelchairs with special balloon tyres – a much easier way to get closer to the waterside. They are available to hire from the beach offices.

What to look out for
You will always see plenty of seagulls on the beach front, waiting for the opportune moment to steal someone lunch!

There are always lots of boats and yachts out on the water, including the bigger carriers that travel from Poole to Guernsey, Jersey and Cherbourg.

WALK 8
Bournemouth Pier to Coy Pond

This is a fantastic walk through the lower, central and upper gardens of Bournemouth, following the Bourne Stream into Coy Pond. There is an abundance of wildlife, flora and fauna throughout, which is remarkable considering that the walk takes place in the heart of Bournemouth.

Although the walk is quite long, the terrain makes it effortless whether you are using a pushchair or a wheelchair. You also have the option of reducing the length of the walk by simply crossing through the gardens on one of the

Distance	4.4 miles (7.14 km)
Parking	There is a car park on Bath Road next to the Royal Bath, De Vere Hotel, the postcode is BH1 2EW – charges apply. There are 7 designated disabled parking spaces. There is plenty of additional parking in the Pavilion car park, directly over the road. As you come into Bournemouth, follow the signs for the beachfront and the Bournemouth International Centre (BIC), the car park is approximately 150 meters before the BIC
Facilities	Toilets (with a baby change station and a fully accessible changing facility and toilet with a hoist), cafes, snack bars, restaurants, bars, benches, bins, dog bins, mini golf, Bournemouth Eye, shops, play park
Gradient	The majority of the walk is flat with a couple of very short sections of inclines and declines
Terrain	Tarmac, small concrete section and gravel around Coy Pond (which can be avoided)
Map	OS Explorer OL22

many designated paths and joining the returning path that takes you back to your start point.

The Area

Bournemouth is one of Britain's most popular seaside resorts and the walk through the heart of Bournemouth is a real delight in very season. The gardens themselves are grade 2 listed in the English Heritage Register of parks and gardens and Bournemouth are exceptionally proud of them.

The Victorian gardens are separated into three sections, each one a delight to explore. The lower gardens are most often used for fun and activities, while the central and upper gardens retain a more natural feel.

The Walk

This walk start at the Bournemouth Pier, so with your back to the sea, walk under the concrete bridge and take the path to the left. The permanent snack booth will then be on your right as you pass by. Follow this wide path and walk towards the Band Stand, which will be in your line of sight and positioned on the other side of the stream and green area. As you continue on this path you will be walking towards Bournemouth town centre and in the distance you will see a church spiral to your left.

You will pass the miniature golf centre on the left and past the huge Bournemouth Balloon on your right. Throughout the gardens there are plenty of places to stop and rest on benches or even on the grass. In the summer months, residents and tourists alike will come here to enjoy the atmosphere and the sunshine.

Just before you reach the shopping centre, you will walk past a brown building on the left, which is the toilet block and has a baby change station as well as a fully accessible changing/toilet facility with a hoist. Walk up the concrete slope and cross over the road. You now need to head to the left of the café in front of you and walk up past the shops. Use the pedestrian crossing on the right to cross the road.

Head right until you find the entrance to the gardens. There will be a signpost pointing to the left, saying 'Coy Pond via Gardens'. Pass the large white war memorial on your right and continue on until you reach the Jurassic Play Jungle on your left. You will now need to head diagonally towards the right and join the pedestrian and cycle path, the tennis courts will be on your right.

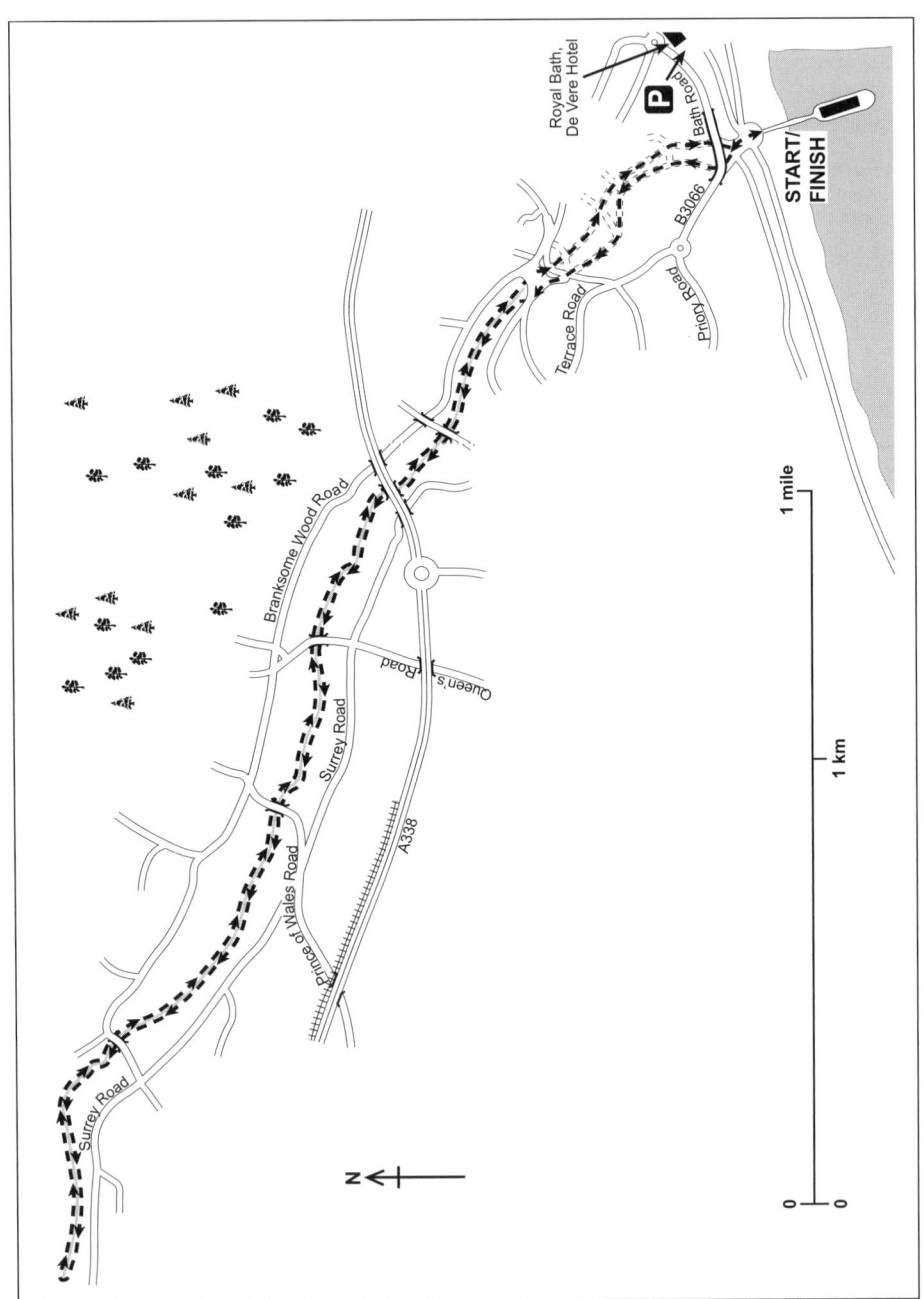

Walk underneath the bridge and then leave the cycle and pedestrian path, use the path immediately next to the wall, which takes you into the gardens and closer to the stream. This is ideal if you enjoy the sound of water as you can often here the stream babbling away when the water levels are high. At the end of this path, it will join up with the cycle path and you will head right.

Cross over the one-way road (looking to the right) and join the cycle track ahead of you. You will eventually come to another one-way road and you need to cross over, checking traffic this time from the left. As you walk through the upper gardens you will notice two boardwalks, these have been placed there to allow people to get closer to the flora and fauna. You will also pass a water Tower that was constructed in approximately 1893.

Keep on the main path until you reach Branksome Wood Road and then cross over into Coy Pond. Walk along this gravel path until you reach a T Junction and then head right, following the gravel path until you see an exit to the road on the left. Cross over the road to Coy Pond, which is filled with coy carp and hungry ducks - a great place to stop and rest with children, just bring bread!

Ducks at Coy Pond

When you are ready, cross back over and walk along Coy Pond Road until you reach the mini roundabout. Cross over and head back into the central gardens with the stream on your right.

You will soon see a path to your right and this will take you off the cycle path and back down towards the stream. You will eventually rejoin the cycle path and have to go up a short incline, cross over a cycle path running in front of you and then head down a short decline towards the tennis courts.

As you continue on the tennis courts will be on your right. The path will take you past the war memorial again and down to the main road opposite shops, restaurants and bars. Cross over and head right. You will see the entrance to the lower gardens in front of you and you now need to retrace your steps back to the bandstand. When the path forks just past the bandstand, take the path to the left towards the pavilion building and after passing this you will see the pier in front of you.

What to see and do

The pier has a host of attractions to offer including the usual seaside pier amusements and rides.

There is a quaint bird aviary and art gallery behind the bandstand, both are free to look around. There is also a snack bar with seating.

In the lower gardens you could play a round of miniature golf and if you are feeling really brace you could go up in the Bournemouth Balloon. The Balloon does allow for a lightweight wheelchair and its special design ensures that viewing is not obstructed.

In the summer months the lower garden is host to a variety of activities, including performances from the bandstand and shows from the nearby dance centre. The colourful lights are a permanent feature of the gardens and in summer they also use little candles to light the path through the lower gardens.

What to look out for

This is part of a designated tree trail and you will find at least 12 different types of tree, including redwood, birch, cypress and palm trees.

With so many trees here the gardens are full of animals, birds and insects. Look out for gulls, mallards, woodpeckers, pigeons, grey wagtail and bats. You will also be surrounded by a large amount of squirrels, they are not afraid of approaching people and are always curious to see if you have any snacks or treats for them.

WALK 9
Poole Park Boating Lake

Poole Park can be found in the centre of Poole and covers 109 acres. It was originally opened in 1890 by the Prince of Wales and was situated on land donated by the Lord Wimborne.

Distance	1.3 miles (2.03km)
Parking	There are several free car parks within Poole Park and on street parking. You will also find allocated disabled spaces in all the car parks and on the roadside near to the main building. Time restrictions do apply and these vary according to where you have parked. For Sat Nav users, the postcode for the park is BH15 2SF. There are three entrances to the park; where Sandbanks Road joins Parkstone Road, from Kingland Road and also along Whitecliffe Road
Facilities	Toilets (there is a accessible toilet which requires a RADAR key, at the café and at the West Gate – restricted opening hours), café, restaurant, snack bars, miniature railway, land train, soft play, ice-skating, play parks (one with a sandpit, so bring a bucket and spade!), go-karts, boats, mini golf, model yachts and tennis. There are plenty of benches and bins throughout.
Gradient	Flat
Terrain	Tarmac, gravel and a couple of concrete sections
Map	OS Explorer OL15

The park is a favourite for walkers, cyclists, runners, dog walkers and those who simply want to enjoy the peace and tranquillity.

The Area

Over half of the 109 acres is covered in water and is home to a variety of wildlife and birds. Excitingly for bird enthusiasts, a number of rare birds have now been spotted in Poole Park, such as the Long-billed Dowitcher, Ring-billed Gull and the Black-tailed Godwit.

Throughout this walk you will come across several sites filled with fitness equipment. This route is a local fitness trail and often used by runners and those who enjoy circuit training.

There really is something here for people of all ages and once you have completed the gentle walk around the boating lake, you can take advantage of some of the parks many facilities.

The Walk

The walk starts by the car park in front of the Seven Boats Restaurant. Here you will also find snack bars offering various refreshments.

Path at Poole Park

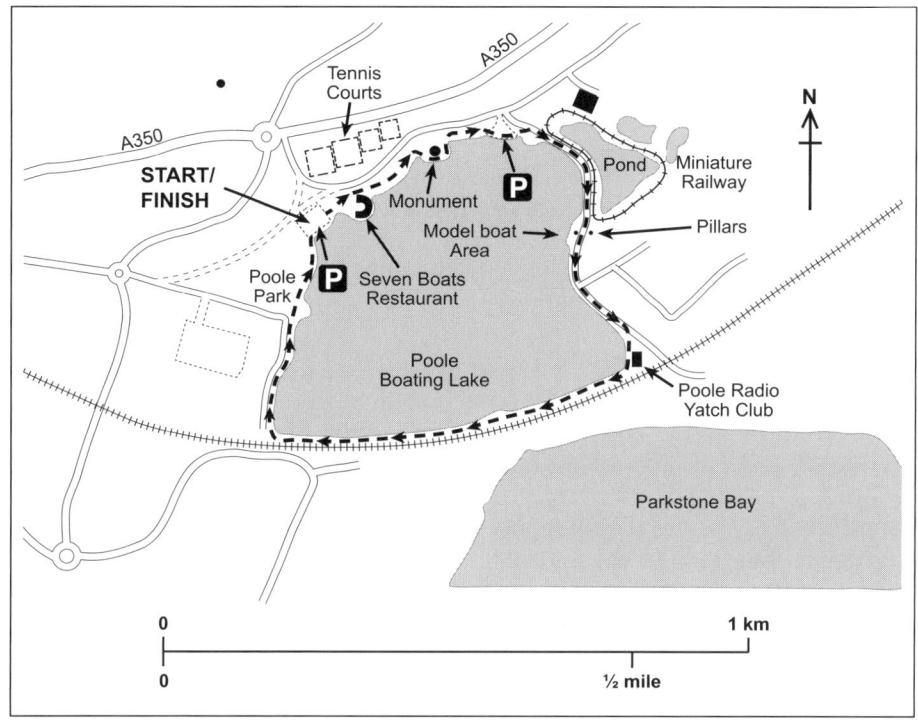

Starting from the lakeside with the Seven Boats Restaurant on your right, head in a clockwise direction. This tarmac path will take you towards a tall monument situated in an elevated garden area. On your left you will see the tennis courts, which are always very well used in good weather.

As there are steps going up to the monument, you will need to follow the path around the boating lake edge and back onto the main tarmac path. You will now be walking towards an alternative car park. Cross the car park and onto the pavement. At this point the walk will be taking you around to the right and around the lake.

You will be able to see on your left a huge pond filled with hungry ducks, Canada geese and swans – a great place to stop and feed the ducks. There is also a children's play park with a sand pit, a miniature railway, ice-skating, soft-play and restaurant facilities. At the back of this building there are also some toilets.

As you walk around the lake you will see the pillars of Poole Park in front of you, you will be going past these and you will now have residential homes on the left and on the right an enclosed section of the lake which is used for remote controlled yachts.

As you come to the end of the boating lake you will see a wooden building which is Poole Radio Yacht Club, you will need to walk on the gravel path in front of this building, which will allow you to continue your walk around the lake. As you continue walking you will be able to look back across the lake and see the Seven Boats restaurant, which was your starting point.

As you walk down this stretch of gravel path you will see the elevated train track to your left, there are often trains travelling from Bournemouth to Poole and seeing the trains go by, is always an added bonus for children. This section of the walk can often have big puddles in wet weather, which is fantastic if kids have wellingtons on for a puddle walk – just be prepared to get a bit damp! Continue walking over the short tarmac area, which is actually a bridge and back on to the gravel path.

Follow this path around the lake until you join a concrete section of the path, this will then take you in front of residential houses that overlook the lake. The path will then return to tarmac and take you to the edge of Poole Park and another children's play park. From here you will be able to see the Seven Boats restaurant and your starting point.

What to see and do
There are plenty of open grass areas for picnic and ball games. There is also a cricket pitch the on the other side of the café and soft play building, which can be used for ball games when matches are not being played. The track around the cricket pitch is a popular place for young children to practice their biking or scooting skills.

The facilities for all the family at Poole Park really are very good and even though the walk is only just over a mile, the other activities on offer will still allow for a great family trip out.

What to look out for
There are ducks, swans, Canada geese, pigeons and seagulls to spot, as well as some of the rarer birds mentioned above. The birds are very used to having people around and you often find the swans just lying down in the middle of the path while people walk by. The park also has plenty of squirrels.

WALK 10
Poole Quay Trail

This is an easy walk alongside the Quay and around Parkstone Bay. With such amazing views out across the water and with easy access for all, this path is well used by walkers, runners, cyclists, wheelchair users and dog owners.

Distance	3.7 miles (6 km)
Parking	There is parking at Poole Quay multi storey car park and they have 6 designated disabled spaces – for Sat Nav users the postcode is BH15 1SB. As you travel into Poole on the A350, follow the brown tourist signs for Poole Quay visitors. There are several car parks to choose from, however the one mentioned above is the closest to the quayside
Facilities	Toilets, including accessible toilets with RADAR keys available at various points of the walk (Poole Quay, Baiter Park and Whitecliff Park) cafes, restaurants, pubs and snack bars - what could be better than warm fish and chips after a long walk! There are also plenty of bins, dog bins and benches on the route
Gradient	Mostly flat, with a couple of undulating areas
Terrain	Mainly smooth tarmac, with a couple of patches of cobbled stones and paving stones
Map	OS Explorer OL15

The Area
Poole is one of the worlds largest natural harbours and is truly magnificent to explore. There is an abundance of wildlife, from birds of international and national importance, to worms and crabs nesting in the wet sand, There are also far reaching views across the water to various islands, including Brownsea and Green Island. All have a very different and interesting story to tell!

The Walk
Starting from the multi storey car park, cross over Stand Street and head down towards the quayside, you will then be heading left. You will see a new development of shops and restaurants on your left, with the quayside on your right.

Walk past the new development and towards the hotel, which will be on your right. Follow this path along the Quay and towards the Lifeboat Museum. Walking around the museum the terrain changes to a cobbled path and paved brick, the path has a very slight slope. Along this stretch of the walk you will be able to see views towards Brownsea Island and in the distance you will see the skyline of Sandbanks. This is reported as being the fourth most expensive place to live in the world.

Poole Quay

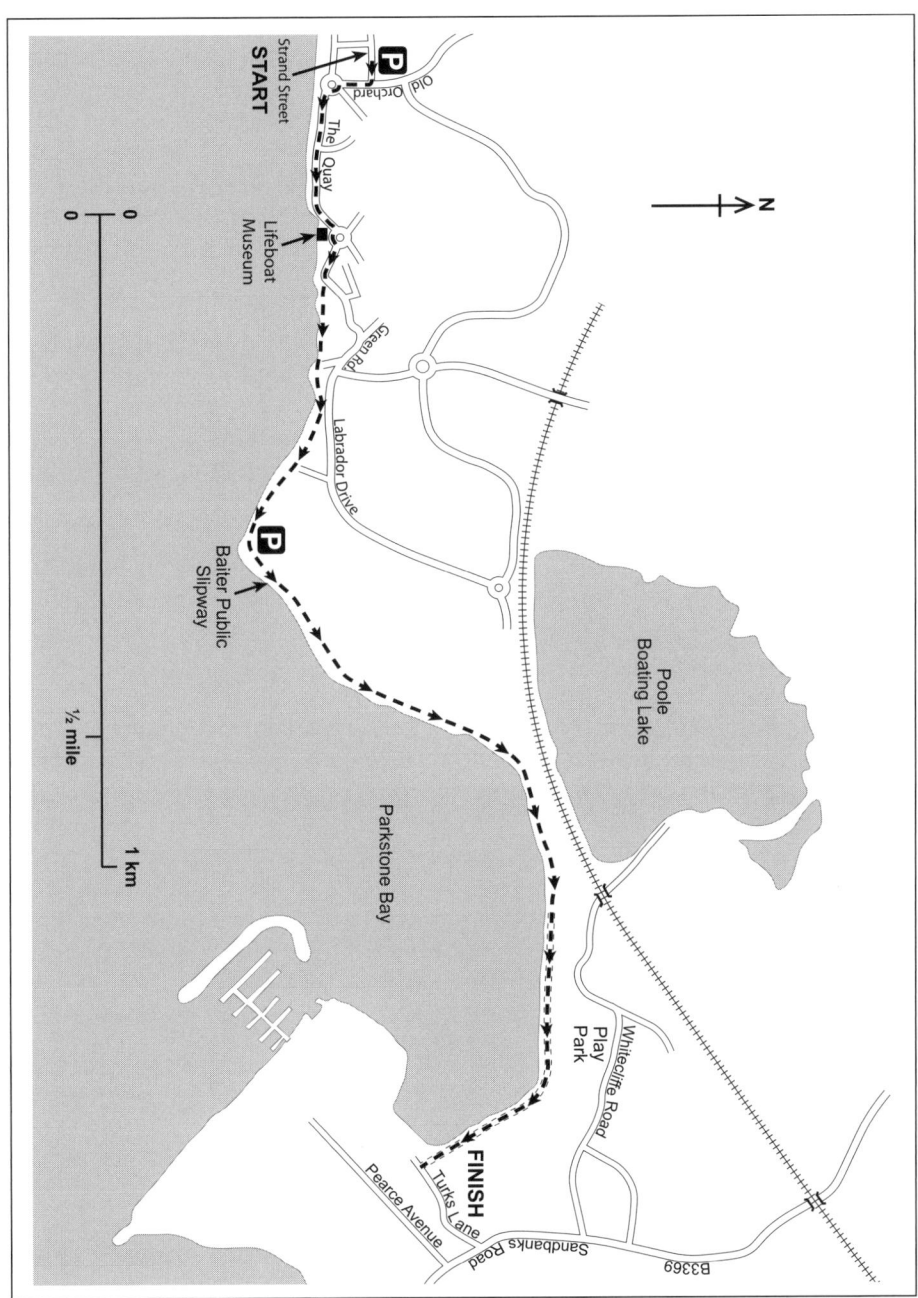

Just past the museum you will take the path that goes along by the waterfront, this is a designated walking path, however cyclists can also use this route. You will walk past a small strip of beach, which is made up of sand and pebbles. There is always a fair bit of seaweed to spot here too!

When you reach the car park on the right, continue straight on. There is a toilet block to the left if needed, however on inspection there was no baby changing station. There is also a huge green area to the left here, which is ideal for picnics and ball games.

As you continue walking around the green you will come to 'Baiter Public Slipway' on your right. In nice weather this is a very well used slipway.

In the distance and to your left you will see the train track and on the other side of this is Poole Boating Lake. As you walk on you will then see a play park on the left, a great place for children to play, while you take a break.

The path then takes you into Parkstone Bay Local Nature Reserve, which is a Site of Specific Scientific Interest and hence is a specially protected area. It is important for the national survival of 12 species of birds and a further 2 more are of international importance.

As you continue walking around the bay, the path will take you right to 'Turks Lane' road. Here you need to stop and retrace your steps back to Poole Quay and the start of the walk. There are more toilet facilities in the white building to your left as you face the road.

What to see and do
Kids will love to look at the collection of boats that are moored in Poole Harbour. They will be able to see everything from the giant Condor Ferry and huge extravagant Sunseeker Yachts to smaller sailing boats.

Early in the morning you can often spot fishermen trying to catch fish, or people with buckets crabbing in the wet sand.

To make a real day of it you could even consider a boat trip around the Quay to get a closer view of some of the islands, or simply to experience the wind in your hair and sprays of salt water on your face – lovely!

What to look out for
This walk is fantastic for spotting an array of birds, especially as the site is designated as a place of scientific interest. You will see many bird lovers with

their binoculars trying to catch a glimpse of the birds with international importance.

Team of volunteers regularly count the birds in the harbour, it is estimated that there are in excess of 20,000 birds here in winter. If you are lucky you may be able to spot an Oyster Catcher, Redshank, Turnstone or Dunlin.

WALK 11
Upton Country Park

This beautiful award-winning park is set in over 100 acres. With its fantastic gardens, woodlands and shorelines, it truly deserves the accolades of being one of the best green spaces in the country.

This is a fairly easy walk through the country park and due to the abundance of wildlife it is a great walk for children who are enthusiastic about wildlife.

Distance	1.9 miles (3.13km)
Parking	As you travel from Poole on the A350 towards the A35, you will see brown tourist signs that will direct you straight to Upton Country Park - the postcode is BH17 7BJ. There are plenty of parking spaces available and the best place to park is by the main toilet block. Parking is free and there are no time restrictions. There are no designated disabled parking spaces; however finding somewhere appropriate to park should be very easy
Facilities	Toilets, with baby change and accessible toilets available for those with a RADAR key both in the car park and by the tearooms. There is also a gallery, education centre, benches, dog bins and general bins throughout.
Gradient	Mainly flat with a few sections of inclines and declines
Terrain	Woodland, concrete, tarmac and grass. A couple of short muddy sections which when wet could be a challenge to wheelchair users
Map	OS Explorer OL15

The Area
Situated just four miles from Poole centre, it is a rare treat to find such an amazing green space so close to a large town. It is very well looked after and maintained and as such it is true delight to walk around.

The Upton Country House was once the centrepiece of the Upton Estate and as such is an impressive and imposing Georgian, Grade 2, listed building, built in 1818.

The Walk
Starting from the main car park by the toilet block, follow the one-way system to the far end of the car park. As the road starts to loop around, you will see a gravel track to the left, take this path.

You will shortly come to a signpost and T Junction; here you will head right, which is signposted 'Grove Wood and Hamworthy'. This stretch of path before the large metal gate can get very muddy in wet weather, however the rest of the walk is much firmer under foot. Go through the smaller wooden gate on the right hand side.

The terrain then becomes concrete, however in autumn this can be covered with leaves that are slippery when wet. The path is very wide and straight here and it makes a great place for children to run and cycle ahead and explore. Take care here as the path initially has a very slight decline.

When you come across a path to the right with a woodland terrain, take a right. Ahead of you is the cycle path, which you can choose to take if you prefer not to take in the small detour. The woodland path is still accessible for an all terrain pushchair, however it is bumpy in places due to tree roots and may be best avoided if you are in a wheelchair. Continue walking along this woodland path, until you come to a dog bin on the left and a long board walk to the right. This is a great place to let children get really close to the wildlife and the surrounding heath land.

After you have finished exploring keep walking on this woodland path until you pass the pond on your right. You will shortly rejoin the main concrete walkway and cycle path and will head right. This is where the path meets up if you had chosen not to do the woodland detour.

You will now be walking down a straight path, passing the pond on your right. After approximately 200 meters take the turning on the left, which is sign

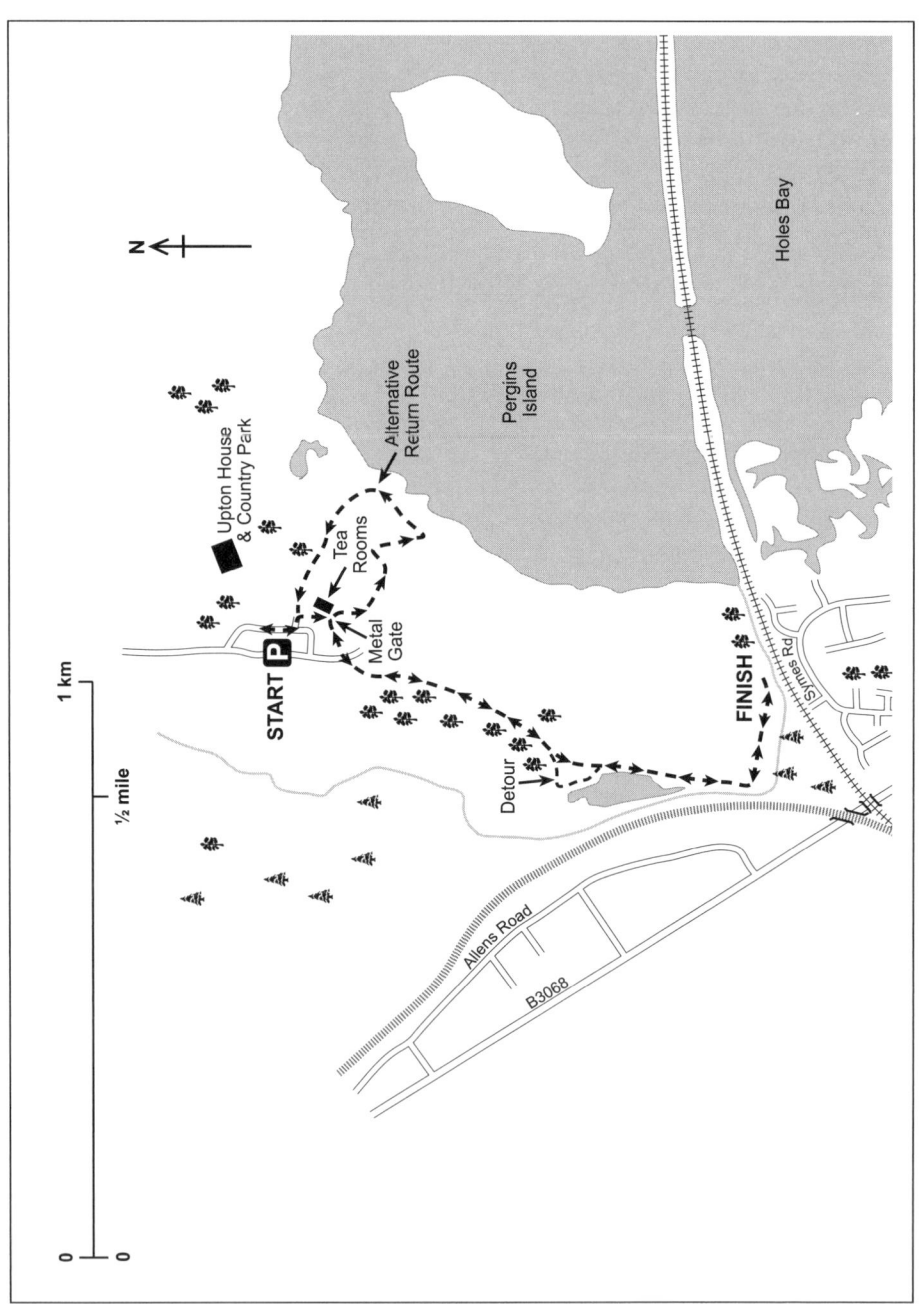

posted to 'Symes Road'. This track takes you around the perimeter of the field and you will notice a stream on the right. You will soon reach a tall metal gate and it is here that you will need to turn around and retrace your steps back towards the car park.

As you approach the gate that takes you back to the car park and the main complex, there is a slight incline. When you have gone through the metal gate, continue straight on following the signs for the 'Tea Rooms' and 'Gallery'. When you reach the T Junction there will be another signpost in front of you and this time you head right towards the 'Toilets' and 'Walled Gardens'.

The toilets and café are on your left and you will now be walking towards the walled gardens. They are only open at certain times of the year, but are full of vibrant colours in the summer. Walk past the plant centre on your left and over the green area. There are plenty of benches here to stop and enjoy the views. After crossing the grass, rejoin the main pathway. To the left you will see a covered area for several benches and you will be turning right heading down towards the shoreline.

Path at Upton Country Park

The path has a gentle decline down to the shoreline and the bird hide. This is a great place to see what birds you can spot and the hide has been made fully accessible. If you choose not to stop at the bird hide, follow the path around to the left and you will see that you are looping around and heading back up to the walled gardens. Take the path immediately to the left and walk through the trees, straight up towards the main walkway.

When you reach the top of this slight incline, turn right and keep on the path that takes you alongside the walled gardens and then past a large building on the left. This is actually the gallery and café area. In front of you will be the car park and the starting point of your walk.

What to see and do
There is a fantastic educational centre, which really makes the most of the safe outdoors area for teaching children about wildlife and giving them the chance to get close to wildlife.

The accessible bird hide is a great place to look at birds on the mudflats and in the marshes.

If you have older children with you who enjoy biking, this is a great place to build confidence on terrain other than tarmac.

What to look out for
Over 150 species of birds have been sighted in the park and your sightings will depend on the time of year. We visited in late summer and we were able to spot and identify, Mallards, Black-headed Gulls, a Chaffinch and Sparrows. A bird-spotting book would be very handy as many of the birds were unknown to me.

Watch out for the squirrels in autumn that are stocking up for winter.

WALK 12
Old Harry Rocks

This is a lovely walk that takes you from Studland village to Old Harry Rocks. The views across the Studland Bay and out over the English Channel are far-reaching and breathtaking. Bournemouth, Hengistbury Head and even the Isle of Wight can be seen from here.

The walk does have a few inclines and declines that you will need to navigate, but nothing that was a real struggle for either me, or the all-terrain

Distance	2.6 miles (4.12 km)
Parking	There is a National Trust car park at the start of the walk, with allocated disabled spaces - charges apply unless you are a National Trust member. The Sat Nav code is BH19 3AU. As you travel towards Studland on the Ferry Road (B3351) you will see a road on the left, directly after the Studland Riding Stables on your right, called Beach Road. As you follow this road around it will lead into Manor Road and this is where you will find the National Trust car park on your right just before the public house
Facilities	Pub, toilets (no baby change or disabled facility), bins, dog bins
Gradient	There is a relatively steep decline on the tarmac road at the start of the walk and then a steady incline at the start of the track leading to Old Harry Rocks. The majority of the walk is then flat with a few gentle inclines
Terrain	Gravel, tarmac, grass and cobbled stone.
Map	OS Explorer OL15

pushchair. *Due to the rain there are several sections that can get quite muddy and bumpy. The path is suitable for all-terrain wheelchairs or trampers and those who are confident with more challenging terrains, but I would not recommend attempting this with a standard wheelchair.*

The Area
Old Harry Rocks is one of Dorset's most famous landmarks and as such attracts many visitors each year. The striking cliffs are made from white chalk and are extremely impressive to look at. The rocks have gained their shape due to the action of the waves over many hundreds of years. The relentless motion of the sea means that the cliffs are under constant threat of erosion and hence the rocks will forever change their shape.

The path is very popular with other walks, dog owners, cyclists and horse riders.

The Walk
From the National Trust car park, turn right and head down the road, walking past the Public House on your right. Shortly after the Public House the road will take you down a steep decline, as it is on tarmac it will not cause you any

Bankes Arms Country Inn, Studland

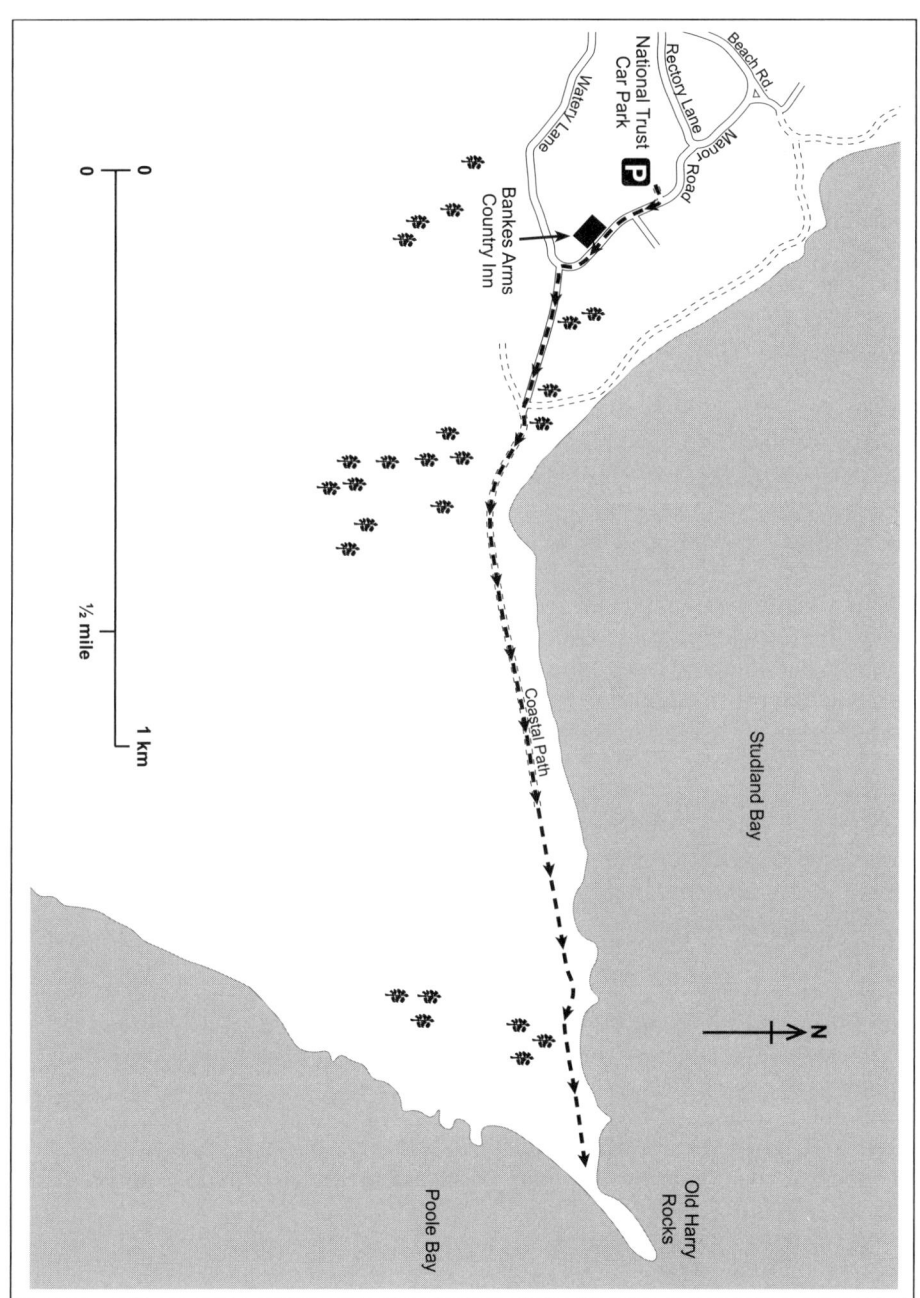

issues, just be sure to keep a firm grip on your pushchair or wheelchair! You will walk past a wooden gate on the left with a path that takes you down to the beach and then you will come to a white toilet block. Just in front of this building, you will see a track to the left and a signpost saying 'Costal Path - Old Harry Rocks'.

Take this path up the steady incline and you will now find that the terrain changes to broken tarmac and cobbled stones, this is due to erosion over time and tree roots coming through the path. Please do not be put off by the terrain here, it is a very short section and although bumpy it is still easy enough to navigate over. This is the only part of the walk where the terrain is like this.

The path will shortly even out and the terrain will become much easier to navigate over. Walk past the black gates on the left and you will now have fields to your right. As you continue on, you will come across a path to the left, however you need to keep going, once again there is a signpost to 'Old Harry Rocks' directing you straight on.

The path starts to become very wide and you will have more fields to the right. There are some great places along this stretch of the walk to play in puddles when it has been raining, just make sure you have your wellingtons on! As the path starts to open up you will have great views of the sea to your left and you will even be able to hear the waves crashing against the shoreline. As you look out to sea, you will have fantastic views of Sandbanks and Poole.

The terrain will then become grass and you will be able to see tracks in the grass where permitted vehicles have driven. The grass is very easy to navigate over and because the track is so wide and long, children can have a great time running ahead while still being in your sight.

At the end of this long grass section, the track turns back to a gravel path and takes you on a slight incline. You will walk through a wooded area and shortly the path will start to head towards the left, you will be able to see the sea and Old Harry Rocks directly in front of you.

This section of the walk has wide grass verges, but does not have a fence between the path and the cliff edge, so please take care with dogs and children who go off and explore.

Once you reach Old Harry Rocks, this is where the walk ends. When you have taken in the views and rested you will then need to turn around and retrace your steps.

What to see and do
It is hugely therapeutic to watch the waves crash against the shoreline by Old Harry Rocks and when the wind is up it is very easy to see how the waves can cause erosion of the rocks. The sea is an exceptional colour of turquoise here and it definitely reminded me of more exotic shores!

By Old Harry Rocks, there is a huge green area, ideal for picnics and enjoying the views back towards Bournemouth, Hengistbury Head and the Isle of Wight. Just keep an eye on inquisitive children and dogs near the cliff edges!

What to look out for
From Old Harry Rocks you can see plenty of boats and yachts in the water.

Cows and horses can be found in the meadows and fields alongside the track. Black-backed Gulls are very common here and Peregrine falcons can sometimes be seen, swooping down to catch their prey.

There is a variety of hedgerow wildlife, in particular an array of beautifully coloured butterflies, such as the Adonis Blue and the Chalkhill Blue.

Old Harry Rocks

WALK 13
Wareham Quay – Frome River Walk

This is a lovely short linear walk to do after having Sunday lunch in one of the many eating establishments around the Wareham Quay, which historically used be a port. The walk takes you down the River Frome to the Yacht Club where you can enjoy looking at all the boats on their way to and from Poole Quay. You can also spend some time exploring the Priory Meadows, which is also completely accessible.

Distance	1.1 mile (1.75 km)
Parking	At the Wareham pay and Display Quay car park, which has an allocated disabled parking space. As you travel into Wareham on the B3075 the Quay can be found off the main road, either just before or just after the bridge, depending on whether you are coming from the North or South. The postcode for Sat Nav users is BH20 4LP. If all spaces have been taken you can park in one of the nearby car parks and walk the short distance back down to the quayside. The town centre car parks do have more allocated disabled parking spaces available
Facilities	Bins, benches, pubs, and cafes in the town and by the quay, toilets in the town centre (Howards Road and at The Quay, a RADAR key is required for the accessible toilet facilities)
Gradient	Flat
Terrain	Tarmac and gravel. The Priory Meadows is gravel and grass with a couple of wooden bridges
Map	OS Explorer OL15

The Area

With its large earth walls surrounding the town, Wareham is one of only two remaining Saxon walled towns in the country. They were built as a defence by King Alfred the Great, who wanted to protect the town against the Vikings.

The Walk

From the quay car park, cross over the bridge and then walk through the metal gate to your left and onto the riverside.

To your right you will see the Priory Meadows, which can be explored for wildlife either before or after you complete the main walk. This is a lovely place to look over the water meadows and to learn more about the wildlife that inhabit the area. Children can run ahead around the circular path with no risk of falling into any water and remain in your line of sight.

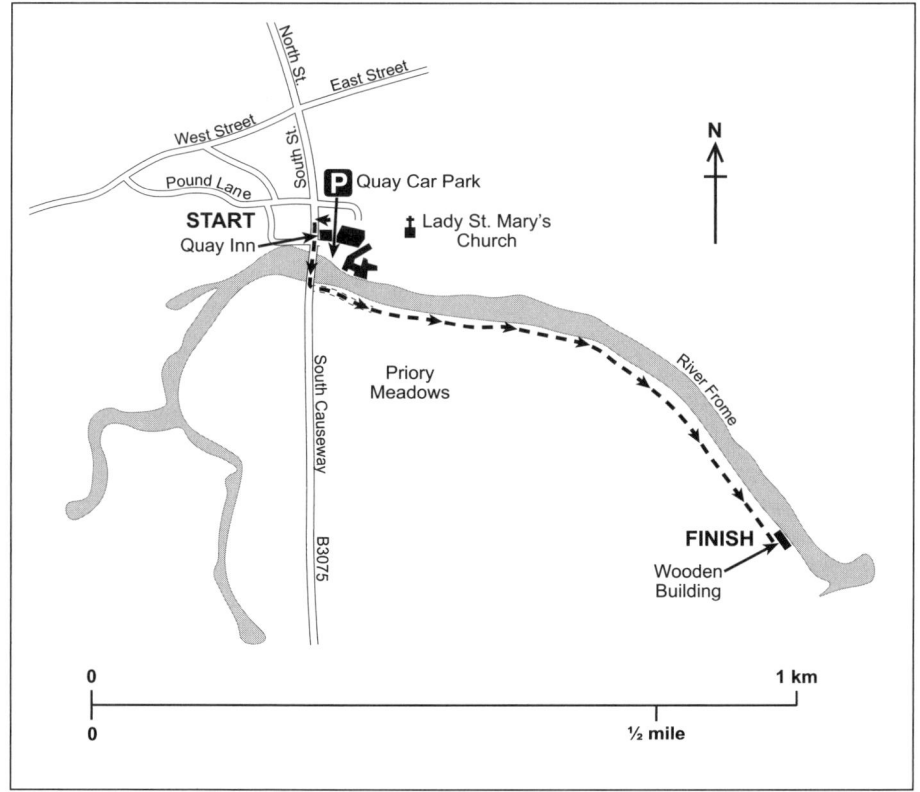

Wareham Quay

Walk along the short section of tarmac path until it turns to a gravel track. To your left you will be able to see the 12th century Lady St Mary's Church and next to this, the Priory Hotel and its exquisite gardens. The Priory Hotel is steeped in history, going back as much as 1300 years. It was once home to monks and nuns, however it is now a privately owned luxury hotel.

As you continue on this track you will notice that the path narrows down slightly, therefore I would not recommend this for a double width buggy. To your right there is a vast expanse of meadows and fields where cows and other farm animals tend to graze.

Along the walk you can see the various access points to the boats and as there is no barrier between the path and the river, it would be wise to keep an eye on adventurous children and dogs!

You will stay on this path for approximately half a mile, until you reach a wooden building, which is part of the Radclyffe Yacht clubs facilities. Here you need to turn around and retrace your steps.

What to see and do
There are always plenty of swans and ducks to feed at the quayside.

For a very special treat you could have afternoon tea at the Priory Hotel and then spend some time exploring the four acres of immaculately kept gardens, that are simply brimming with colour.

What to look out for
There are always a huge collection of yachts and boats of all sizes on the river.

Depending on the time of year, you will find stacks of wildlife, flora and fauna in the Priory Meadows. The information boards provide pictures so that children can clearly see what wildlife lives here and what they can spot.

WALK 14
Lawsons Clump

This is a fantastic circular walk through a beautiful and peaceful forest. The wide gravel paths make this an extremely accessible walk and a thoroughly enjoyable experience for all of the family.

This would be a lovely walk for a sturdy all terrain wheelchair or tramper that is able to deal with woodland tracks.

Distance	3.5 miles (5.68 km)
Parking	There is free parking at Lawsons Clump. There are no designated disabled parking spaces. From Sandford take the B3075, which is Morden Road and signposted to 'Morden' After approximately one mile you will see the Forestry Commission sign for Lawsons Clump on the right
Facilities	Picnic benches and dog bins
Gradient	A few sections that have slight inclines and declines. However the all-terrain pushchair made these short sections very easy
Terrain	Gravel and sandy/woodland tracks
Map	OS Explorer OL15

The Area

This walk is ideal for children who want to run ahead and explore, as they will always be in your line of sight. It is also an ideal place for older children to practice their mountain biking.

The area is very popular with walkers, cyclists, horse riders and dog owners.

The Walk

From the car park you will see a gravel path to the right. Take this path and walk up the hill, past the track on the right, which is actually the end of this circular walk.

You will need to stay on the main track for the duration of this walk and not take any of the alternative tracks to the left or right. The terrain on these alternative tracks can be much more challenging and the route is not always accessible.

You will eventually come to a section of the path where it bends around to the right and you need to follow this path. You will notice a long straight track to the left, which goes down to another car park. After approximately 350 metres you will come to another section of the path where there is a track directly in front of you and the main path bends around to the right. You need to take the path to the right and continue on this looped walk.

You will soon walk past a pond to the right of you, with various tunnels dug out of the ground underneath the fence, allowing dogs easy access to the

The trail at Lawson Clump

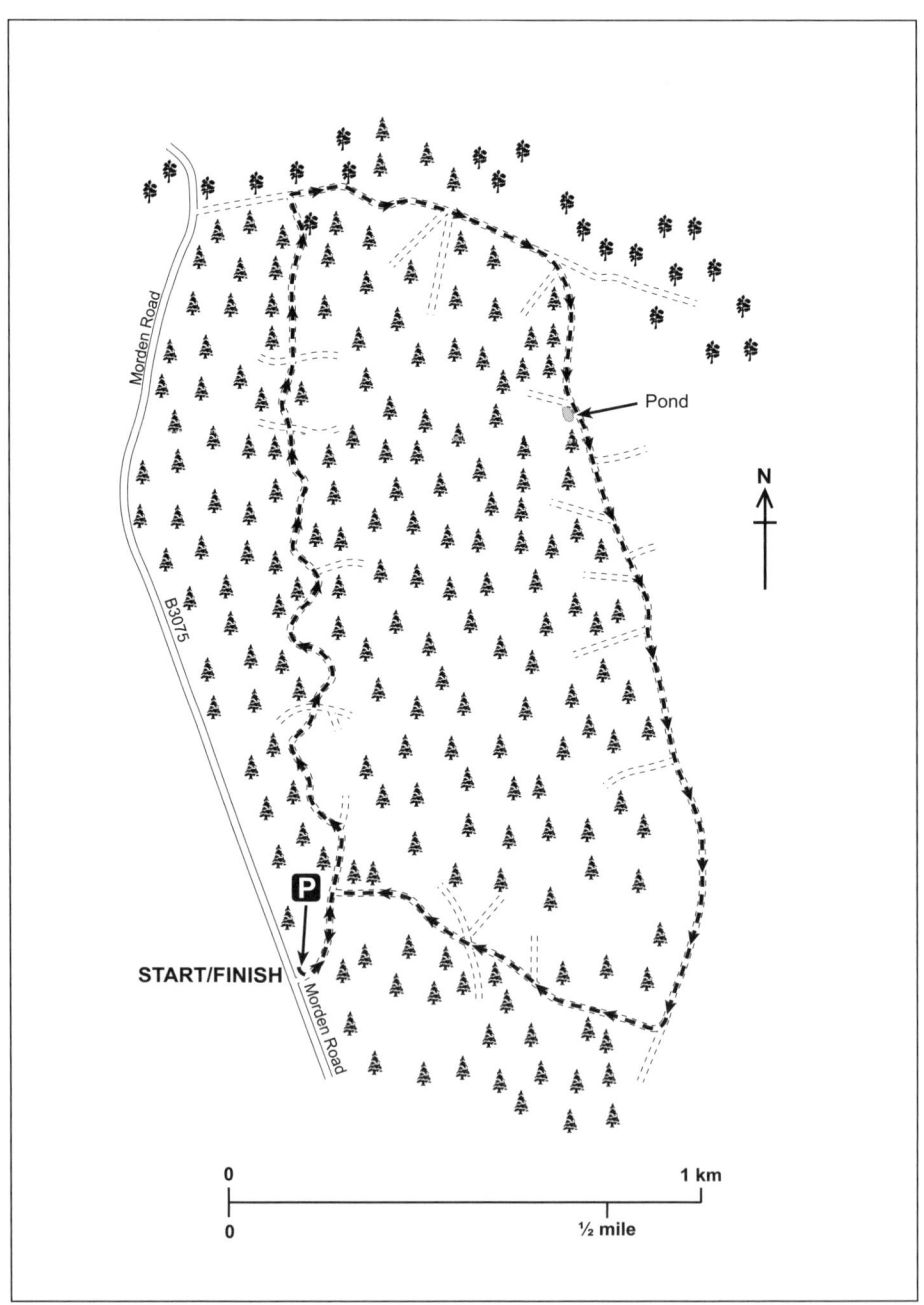

water. However, there were also several drainage tunnels that were filled with dirty water, so take care with children and dogs if you don't want to have a smelly car ride home!

You will come to a section of the path where you have a large expanse of farmland to the left and woodland to the right. You will be walking straight on following the perimeter of the field. Eventually you will come to a section of the walk that has a track with grass growing down the middle of it, continue walking on this path and alongside the edge of the field.

You will notice that to your right the woodland starts to thin out and heath land takes its place. You will come across a path to the right, which is opposite a metal gate with a sign that states 'Private Property, No rights of Way'. You need to turn right here, as the track ahead will simply take you to the main road. There is a gentle incline here and when you get to the top you will see a crossroads where you need to continue straight on. The views at the top here are lovely and if you are lucky enough to catch it when the sun is going down it is truly magical.

As you head down the track you will be able to see the car park to your left. You will come to a T Junction and you will then need to turn left and walk back to the car park and picnic area.

What to see and do
If older children are not keen on walking, why not take their bikes and allow them to practice mountain biking on easy and forgiving tracks.
    There are picnic benches at the start of the walk if you wanted to have refreshments.

What to look out for
There are thousands of pine and fir trees here, as well as hundreds of holly bushes. These look stunning in the colder months, especially when the berries are really radiant and red.
    There are plenty of birds to spot throughout the walk.

WALK 15
Sika Trail

This is part of the Sika Trail, a national cycle route, which takes you through the beautiful woodland of Wareham Forest. This is a lovely walk, however the hill at the end could be very off putting if you are not fit and not prepared for it.

This walk is not for the faint hearted! I would not recommend this walk for any wheelchair users, due to the steep hill at the end

Distance	4.9 miles (7.39km)
Parking	There is free parking at the Sika Trail car park. As you go travel from Sandford towards Wareham on the A351, follow the signs for Bere Regis. This will be sign posted from the first roundabout you reach outside Wareham and the road you need is called 'Bere Road'. After approximately 1 mile on the right you will see the green forestry commission signs for the car park
Facilities	Dog bins, picnic benches, Silent Women public house (just a bit further up Bere road)
Gradient	Mainly flat, there are a couple of places where there are gentle inclines and declines and then there is a short section of approximately 50 metres at the end of the walk, where the hill is very steep
Terrain	Gravel, sandy gravel
Map	OS Explorer OL15

The Area
The Sika Trail takes its name from the sika deer, which can be found throughout the Forest. These deer were first introduced into the UK in 1860 and are now a familiar sight in forests all over the country.

Throughout this walk you will see many tracks going off into the forest or heath land, however many of these alternative routes through the forest are either not accessible for those with access challenges, or will make the walk much more challenging to complete. I would highly recommend staying on the designated track.

There are several drainage ditches on this walk that are filled with dirty water. Take care with children or dogs as you could have wet companions on the way home!

The Walk
With your back to the main road, head left to pick up the start of the walk. Go past the picnic bench and take the wide track to the far left. This will take you straight up to the start of the Sika Trail.

Once you have passed through the gate, you will see that there are two main wide gravel tracks in front of you and a grass path to your right. You need to

The Sika Trail

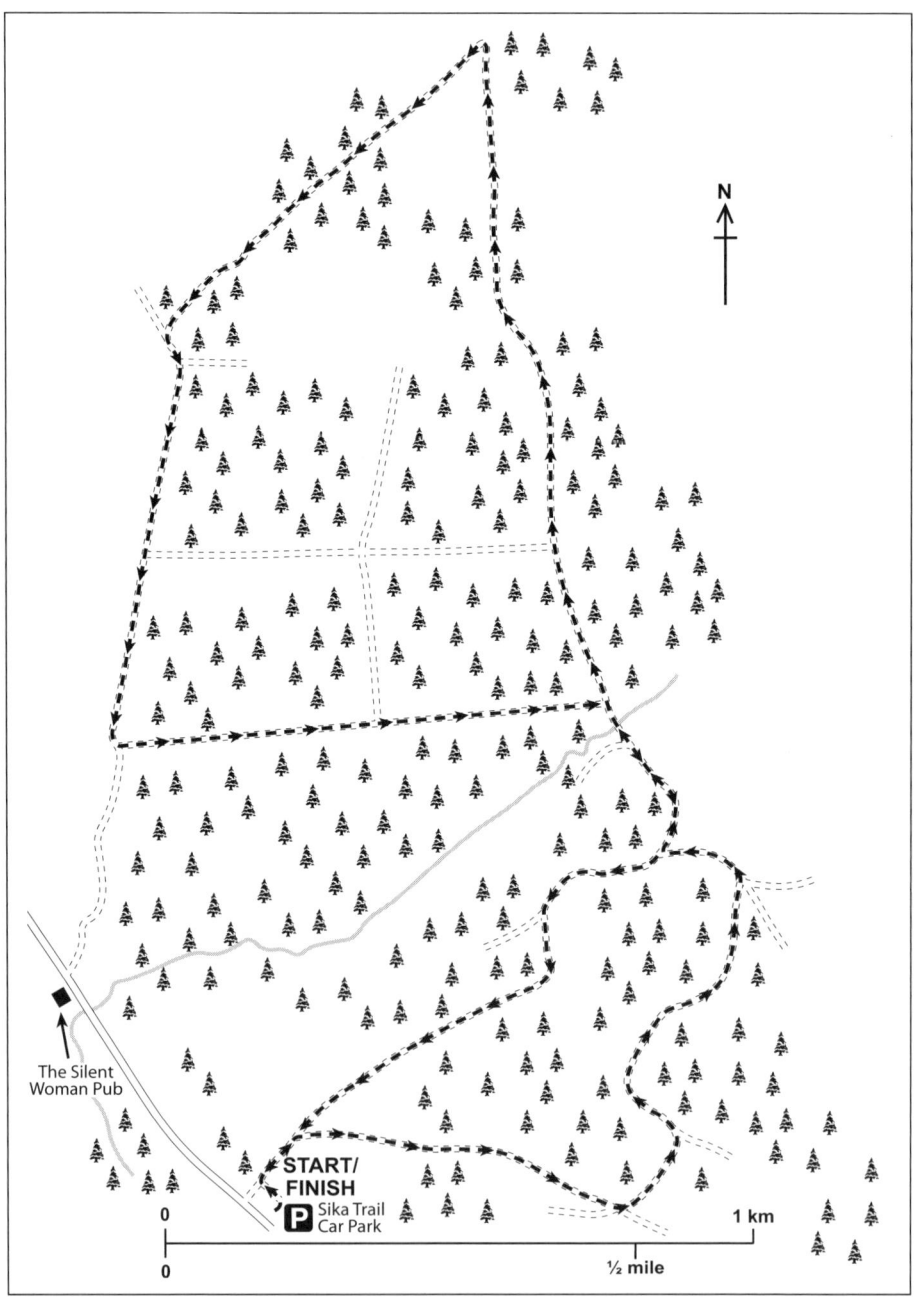

take the gravel path to your right; the left hand path is the end of this circular walk.

When you arrive at the crossroads look to your left and you will see a bench. You will now turn left and continue down the gentle meandering descent. When you arrive at the bottom of the slope you need to follow the path around to the left. This path will shortly meet another track and you will be turning right. The turning to the left is the last section of the walk and also the track before the steep hill. If you preferred an easier (but longer) ascent at the end of your walk, you could retrace your steps back to the car park from this point.

As you continue on this path to the right, you will now have a great expanse of heath land to your right and the forest to your left. This section of the walk will take you straight on for approximately one kilometre.

When you reach the second path on the left you will be able to see 'Parsons Pleasure'. This is a water logged heath land that was once considered the worst in Europe. By conducting an experiment with drainage they were able to make it capable of sustaining plant and tree life again and it has remained as a memory to him ever since.

Keep going straight on until you can see a metal gate directly in front of you. There will be a track that goes straight ahead into the forest, with a sign that states 'Except Emergency Vehicles', you will be looping back on yourself by following the track to the left.

Continue on and you will eventually come to a wooden gate that you need to go through. The main gates on this walk should always be kept open, however if they are closed or locked for any reason, just use the smaller gates to the side.

At the next T Junction take a left and walk through another wooden gate. You will know that you are in the right place, as you will pass two yellow Sika Trail signs with the numbers 28 and 29 on them.

You will pass farms and fields to your right and eventually see a path leading straight through the forest on the left. You need to continue straight up the slight ascent in front of you. The path quickly evens out and you will then come to another path on the left. Take this path through the wooden gate and walk until you reach the main track at the other end.

At the end of this long track, take a right and continue on. You will pass a turning on the left and will recognise this from earlier in the walk. Shortly you will be at the base of the steep hill. Although it looks daunting, it only lasts for about 50 metres and the all-terrain pushchair was more than capable of getting up the hill. At the top you have a viewpoint to the left and if you take the path to the right, it will take you all the way back to the car park and the starting point of the walk.

What to see and do
This is a great place for children to practice mountain biking on a flat terrain. The length of the walk will also ensure that they sleep well.

The views across the woodlands and heath land are amazing and offer many photo opportunities.

What to look out for
Sika and Roe deer live in the forest, although they are generally quite shy and tend to hide away from people.

The forest has many resident birds, including Woodlarks, the Dartford Warbler, the Nightjar and the Stonechat.

WALK 16
Durlston Country Park

This is a stunning linear walk along the coast and cliff tops from Durlston Castle towards the Anvil Point Lighthouse. Although the walk is quite short the terrain and gradients can be challenging at times, however the views are spectacular and it really is worth the effort. There is one very steep hill at the end of this walk, however it can be avoided.

I would not recommend this particular walk to wheelchair users as it is very bumpy in places.

Distance	1 mile (1.63km)
Parking	There is a pay and display car park at Durlston, the postcode is BH19 2JL. As you come into Swanage head through the town centre and then follow the brown tourist signs for Durlston Country Park
Facilities	Bins, benches, picnic benches, toilets in the visitor centre (no baby change), the toilets at the learning centre have a baby change facility, café and restaurant
Gradient	The walk undulates throughout and can be bumpy in places, not ideal for a young baby. There are a few steep sections and one very steep hill at the end of the walk, which can be avoided by retracing your steps
Terrain	Tarmac, gravel, grass and large gravel
Map	OS Explorer OL15

The Area
This stunning park covers 280 acres and is situated in an Area of Outstanding Natural Beauty (ANOB), just to the south of Swanage.

Much of the park is considered a Site of Special Scientific Interest due to the amount and variety of wildlife that resides here. It has won numerous awards, all of which are very well deserved.

The Walk

The walk starts from the front of Durlston Castle, which is now the new visitor centre.

With your back to the castle, head down the tarmac path to the left. The hill here is quite steep but as it is on tarmac it should not pose you any problems with the all-terrain pushchair.

At the bottom of the hill you will turn right, down another decline and this will be sign posted to 'Tilly Whim Caves' and 'The Lighthouse'. Here the terrain turns to a mixture of tarmac and gravel. At the bottom of this section you will see a circular shaped wall and in front of that some information boards about the wildlife that can be found around the park.

In front of Durlston Castle

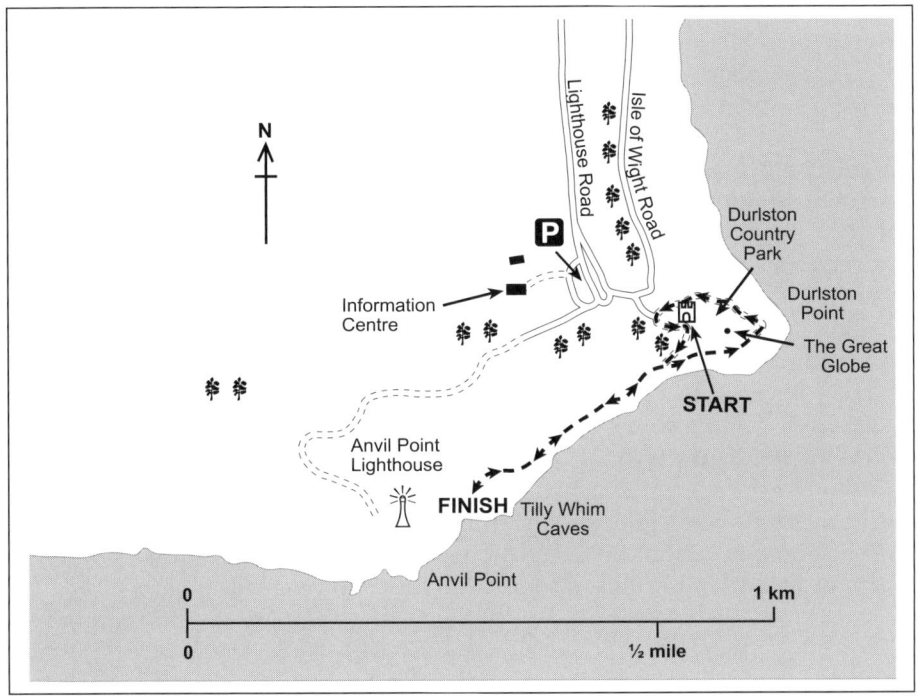

Turn right here and take the coastal path towards the lighthouse. You will now be walking alongside the cliff edge. There is a small stonewall here, which provides a barrier between the path and the cliffs.

On your right you will come across a bird hide which over looks the sea. There is a small step into the hide, but this would be easy for the all-terrain pushchair.

The path then meanders on to the entrance of the now closed, Tilly Whim Caves. These are actually old limestone quarries and were worked in during the 18th century.

This section of the walk ends by the wooden and metal gate, from here you can get some good views of the lighthouse, but the path ahead is totally inaccessible. You will need to retrace your steps back to the information boards at the start of the cliff top walk.

When you reach the information boards you will be continuing straight on around the cliff top, towards 'The Great Globe', which you will see on your left. This is made from forty tons of Portland limestone and is engraved with an 1880's world map.

At this point you have a couple of options for the return journey. If you continue straight on around the coastline, you will have to navigate the steep hill. It is not a short climb and unless you are fit or like a challenge, I would not recommend you attempt this hill. I certainly needed a couple of minutes to get my breath back at the top! If you prefer an easier option I would suggest heading back up the original tarmac path that brought you down to the cliff top. Both routes will take you back to the front of the Durlston Castle and the end of your walk.

What to see and do

Durlston Castle was refurbished in 2011 to provide an engaging visitor centre for both adults and children. There are some interactive things for children to look and play with. The Great Globe in front of the castle was a favourite with our daughter and this garden area is a great place for a picnic.

Cliff top trail at Durlston Country Park

What to look out for
There is an abundance of birds here and it is quite spectacular to watch them soar around the coastline and then land delicately on the cliffs. There are hundreds of colonies here all along the coast for you to observe. We mainly spotted gulls here, although there are many more varieties to see.

The area is also hugely popular for dolphin sightings.

WALK 17
Lodmoor Country Park

Situated to the east of Weymouth this lovely park covers 350 acres and is home to a variety of family attractions, including an RSPB nature reserve. This is an easy circular walk through the country park, taking in the nature reserve. With the huge variety of birds that can be seen here, this is a great educational walk for children.

To make this a circular route, there is a very short section of approximately 250 meters, which requires you to walk on the pavement alongside a main road.

Distance	1.6miles (2.52km)
Parking	You can park at the pay and display car park at the Weymouth Sealife Centre, for Sat Nav users the postcode is DT4 7SX. There are designated disabled parking bays. As you head into Weymouth on the A354, you will come to a large roundabout with a supermarket on your left. Take a left here leaving the main A354 and travel along Dorchester Road. This road will take you right up to the sea front and from here you will head left along Preston Road (A353). If you follow the brown tourist signs for the Sealife Centre and Lodmoor Country Park, you will shortly arrive at the car park
Facilities	Toilets (accessible toilets available and open 24 hours a day, all year round), benches, bins, café, public house, children's park and rides
Gradient	Flat
Terrain	Tarmac, gravel and a wooden bridge
Map	OS Explorer OL15

The Area

Lodmoor Country Park is free to enter; however the additional attractions, i.e. the Sealife Centre and the rides for children are chargeable.

The RSPB Nature Reserve is a wonderful place for getting close to hundreds of birds of differing varieties. It really is a peaceful and tranquil place to walk through.

The Walk

From the car park head into the country park on one of the tarmac paths and walk towards the miniature railway station (Rio Grande), which is over to the left.

From the railway station turn left and this will take you onto a gravel path, which runs alongside the miniature railway track. At the crossroads go straight on and follow this tarmac path clockwise, still alongside the miniature railway track.

You will shortly come to a turning on the left where the path becomes compacted gravel. Take this path and walk down through the trees. You will now have the miniature golf course on your left and a stream to your right.

Path through Lodmoor Country Park

When you come to the next T Junction you will see a bridge to your right, cross over the bridge and then turn right again onto the gravel path. Stay on this main path, ignoring any other tracks to the left and right until you reach the turning on the right, which takes you into the RSPB Nature Reserve. There will be a sign just inside the turning to the track saying that the entrance to the reserve is 800 metres away. You will quickly become surrounded by a variety of bird sounds and you will see birds darting into the reeds and marshlands to either side of you.

Follow the path through the reserve until you reach the other end. Take care with children, as the path is situated right next to the reeds and water. Although the water is not always deep it will disturb the wildlife, especially during nesting periods.

At the end of the path you will exit the reserve and you will now need to head right and cross over the road. Turn left and follow the pavement alongside the main road, all the way back to the car park and your starting point. Once again you will see the brown tourist signs ahead of you, directing you to the car park. This is the only section of the walk that is by a main road. You could

RSPB nature reserve at Lodmoor

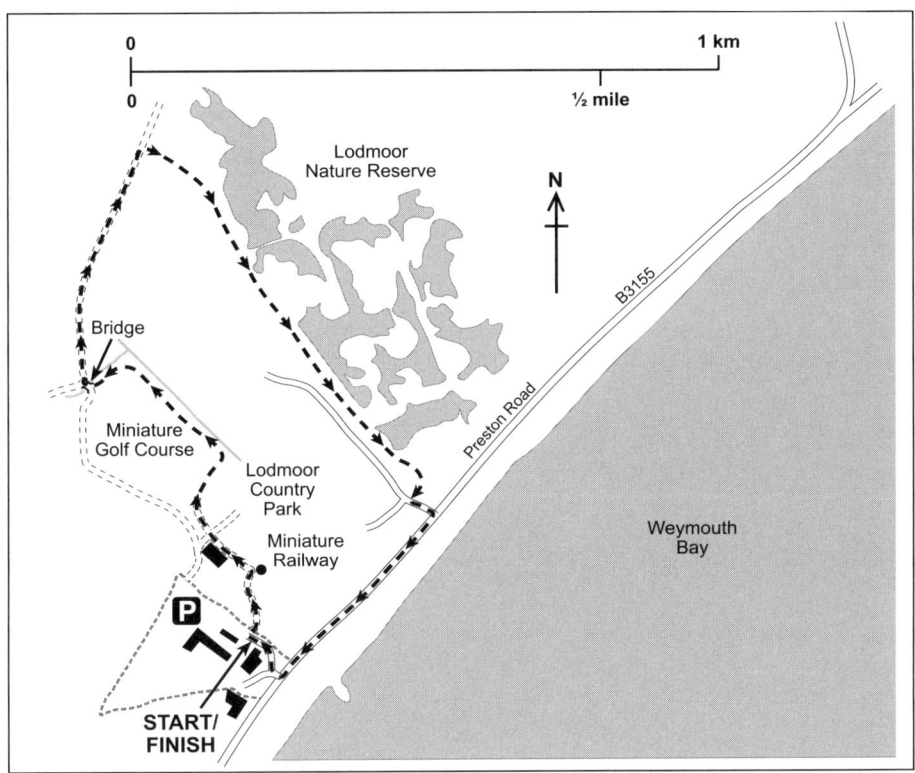

choose to turn around and retrace your steps if you preferred a longer walk and wanted to enjoy the reserve for a second time.

What to see and do
Take some binoculars for older children and go bird spotting on the reserve. There are so many different types of birds here, so a bird watching book will come in very handy!

When it has been raining there will be plenty of puddles along the gravel paths to splash around in.

There are a variety of activities at the country park, i.e. the Sealife Centre, go-karts and the miniature railway.

What to look out for
There are plenty of rabbits throughout the country park and they really don't seem to be very bothered by the presence of people.

You will often see people filming and photographing the birds in the reserve. This is a great opportunity to get really close to these birds and observe them in their natural habit. They have several birds here that are considered star species and they are the Bearded Tit, the Bittern, the Cetti's warbler, the Common tern and the Little egret.

WALK 18
Radipole Nature Reserve

This is a lovely nature reserve located in the heart of Weymouth. It is free to enter but donations are always appreciated by the RSPB so that they can continue with their valuable conservation work.

The firm wide paths around the reserve make this an easy walk to complete.

Distance	1.7 miles (2.78km)
Parking	At the Swannery pay and display car park, postcode DT4 7TY. There are 27 blue badge spaces. You will head into Weymouth on the A354 and then take a left over the bridge onto the A353 just before the harbour. This road will take you toward the train station and a retail shopping complex. You will see the Swannery car park to the left of the Kings Roundabout
Facilities	Toilets in the car park (charges apply), an accessible toilet at the Radipole Discovery Centre and another in the car park (RADAR key required) There is also a café in the Discovery Centre that is fully accessible and benches throughout the walk
Gradient	Flat
Terrain	Gravel, tarmac, a wooden bridge and a section of concrete
Map	OS Explorer OL15

The Area

This is a great educational walk, particularly with the large number of birds that live here. The reserve really does provide a fantastic environment where people can get close to nature and observe wildlife in their natural habitat.

Dogs are welcome here, although they must be kept under control and on the designated paths at all times.

The Walk

From the car park and with the public toilets and main road behind you, head to the back of the car park. Over to the right hand side you will see a white building, which is the visitor centre for the nature reserve.

Starting by the visitor centre and with the building on your left, you will see a path in front of you that leads over a wooden bridge and down through the

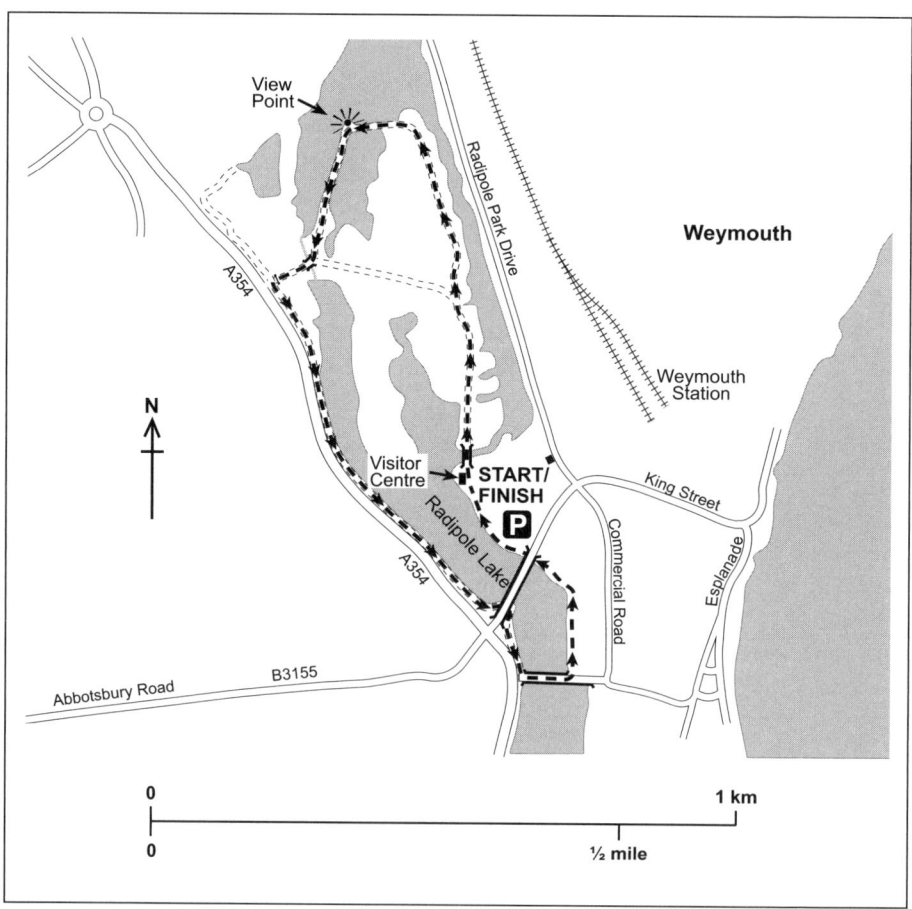

View from Buddlea viewpoint

reserve. Follow this path and you will have wetlands and marshlands either side of you, filled with a variety of wildlife.

When you reach the T Junction, you will need to turn right and this is sign posted 'Buddleia Loop'. As you continue on this path you will see various tracks to the left and right which take you closer to the waters edge and provide a great place to try and spot fish. You will eventually come to the Buddleia viewpoint, where you can look out across the water to the various small islands that have now become home or a resting point for many of the birds.

As you continue on the path you will cross a wooden bridge and arrive at another T Junction, here you will turn right. If you want to make the walk shorter you can turn left here and this will take you back to the visitor centre.

Assuming you have turned right you will see a metal kissing gate in front of you and signs to the right for the North Hide - another great place to get closer to the resident birds and wildlife. Go through the metal kissing gate and then head left, this will take you alongside the water, with the road on your right.

You will eventually go underneath a bridge and you will need to keep walking until you reach the bridge that separates the reserve from the harbour. Cross this bridge and then turn left, you will now be walking down the half cobbled/half tarmac path and back towards your starting point. You will pass a restaurant on the left and a play park on the right.

Walk underneath the bridge and you will find yourself back in the Swannery car park. From here follow the edge of the car park back to the visitor centre where your walk will end.

What to see and do
Bird spotting is hugely popular here for both the beginner and the more experienced bird watcher. The visitor centre is a great resource and is well worth a visit. The staff here are very knowledgeable and helpful – they even have a range of refreshments on offer.

What to look out for
The nature reserve is home to water voles, otters and grass snakes as well as an abundance of insects. We spotted plenty of gulls, mallards and swans, however there are plenty of other birds that regularly make an appearance here, such as the House sparrow, finches, Robins and the Cetti warbler.

WALK 19
Nothe Gardens

This is a fantastic walk around the quiet and tranquil Nothe Gardens, taking in Nothe Fort and the stunning views around the Bay of Weymouth. It also takes you along the sea wall to Newtons Cove. Although this is a short walk, the views that you get to experience from this amazing vantage point are truly wonderful.

The walk can also be adapted so that those in a wheelchair do not have to navigate the gentle inclines. The views are so stunning that a short stroll and a picnic are just as enjoyable.

Distance	1.3 miles (2.15km)
Parking	There are three car parks to choose from, all of which are pay and display. There are plenty of designated disabled parking spaces. Due to the elevated position of the gardens I would not suggest parking in the town and walking up. As you travel on Rodwell Road (A354) head towards the Nothe Peninsula and Portland and you will see brown tourist signs for 'Nothe Fort'. The postcode for Nothe Fort is DT4 8UF
Facilities	Toilets (accessible toilet with RADAR key), café (seasonal), bins and benches
Gradient	Steep in a couple of places, but these sections are short. There are also a couple of gentle inclines
Terrain	Tarmac, gravel and concrete
Map	OS Explorer OL15

The Area
Nothe Fort was built in 1860 as part of the defence of Portland Harbour and is situated at the entrance of Weymouth Harbour. During 1905 and 1938 Nothe Fort was considered an important part of the defence of Portland Harbour, especially as this became the main base for the channel and Atlantic fleets.

In 1956 the fort was no longer used for costal defence and in 1961 it came under the ownership of the Weymouth and Melcombe Regis Borough Council.

The Walk
The walk starts from the car park in the lower part of the gardens opposite Nothe House and a seasonal café. To your left you will have information boards about the area and steps that lead down to the harbour side.

With your back to the car park and with the information boards on your left, take the path directly in front of you. This will take you past a large stone on your right, with the words 'Elizabethan Way' carved into it.

You will see a building in front of you and to the right and this is the toilet block. Stay on the main path and walk towards Nothe Fort, ignoring any paths

Nothe Fort (FAV)

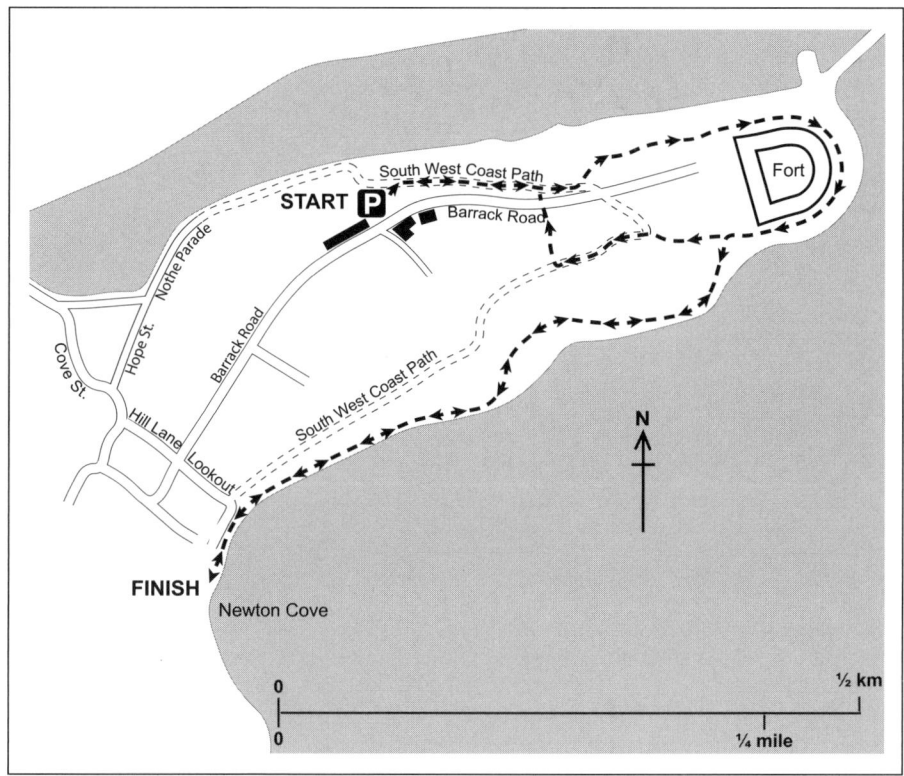

to the left and right. As you look down and to your right you will see a road that leads into the Fort. There are no barriers on the path at this point in the walk, so take care with dogs and children. The path here is also a little bumpy due to tree roots pushing through the pavement.

Follow the path past the fort and around in a u shape until come to a crossroads. The toilet block will now be on your right and a gravel path will be to your left. Walk down the path to the left and then take the second turning on the right, which will take you down closer to the shoreline. This section of the walk is a little steep so do take care.

The views across to Portland are stunning from here and there is a delightful smell of seaweed. The sound of the water lapping against the rocks is very relaxing and therapeutic, it was truly enjoyable to just sit and watch the world

Sea wall to Newtons Cove

go by. As you continue on, take the next path on the left, which takes you down to the sea wall.

Follow the sea wall all the way to the seating area at Newton Cove, where you will turn around and retrace your steps back to the crossroads opposite the toilet block.

When you reach the crossroad again and have the toilet block in front of you, turn left. Then take the path to the right, which cuts across the gardens. Cross the road and rejoin the path, taking you left, back to the start of the walk and the car park.

What to see and do
Take some time out to explore Nothe Fort, which is filled with interesting historical artefacts.

We saw several families exploring the rocks near Newton Cove and looking for resident sea life.

What to look out for
There is a surprising amount of wildlife here. If you are lucky and patient you will be able to spot butterflies, various birds (House Martins, Kestrels and the Black Redstart are regulars here), slow worms and field mice. We also saw many squirrels that were all very friendly and keen to know if you had any treats for them.

There is an array of flora and fauna within the gardens.

WALK 20
Weymouth Harbour Walk

This is an educational linear walk that takes in some fascinating history of Weymouth and its harbour. You do have to walk alongside the main road for approximately a quarter of a mile on the way there and back, but the views of the boats and yachts in the harbour more than make up for this.

As the terrain is mostly tarmac and paved brick, this is an easy walk to complete.

Distance	3 miles (4.90km)
Parking	At the Swannery pay and display car park, postcode DT4 7TY. There are 27 Blue Badge spaces. You will head into Weymouth on the A354 and then take a left over the bridge onto the B3155 just before the harbour. This road will take you toward the train station and a retail shopping complex. You will see the Swannery car park to the left of the Kings Roundabout
Facilities	Toilets in the car park (charges apply and a RADAR key is needed for the accessible facility), cafes, restaurants, pubs, bins and benches
Gradient	Flat
Terrain	Tarmac and patches of paved brick
Map	OS Explorer OL15

The Area
There is such a lot of history connected with Weymouth Harbour, including the interesting plaque fixed into a restaurant wall signalling that in 1348, the

black death had been brought into Weymouth. There was also the royal intervention of Queen Elizabeth I, who settled the disagreements of the two fighting communities, who had argued over the harbour for centuries.

The harbour is still a commercial port and as such vessels will frequently sail over to the Channel Islands. Locally the harbour supports businesses that offer fishing, diving and general boating services to the public.

Weymouth Harbour

The Walk

Starting from the car park and with your back to the toilets and main road head over to the far left side of the car park. You will see a brown tourist sign saying 'Old Harbour', pointing to the left.

This will take you under a concrete bridge and alongside the lake, which will be on your right. You will pass a play area on the left and a restaurant that is based on a boat can be found on the right. As you continue on this path you will shortly come to a bridge, which takes you over the water. Cross here and as you reach the other side turn left towards the harbour.

You will now walk alongside the harbour, which will be on your left and the main road will be on your right. There are plenty of boats and yachts to look

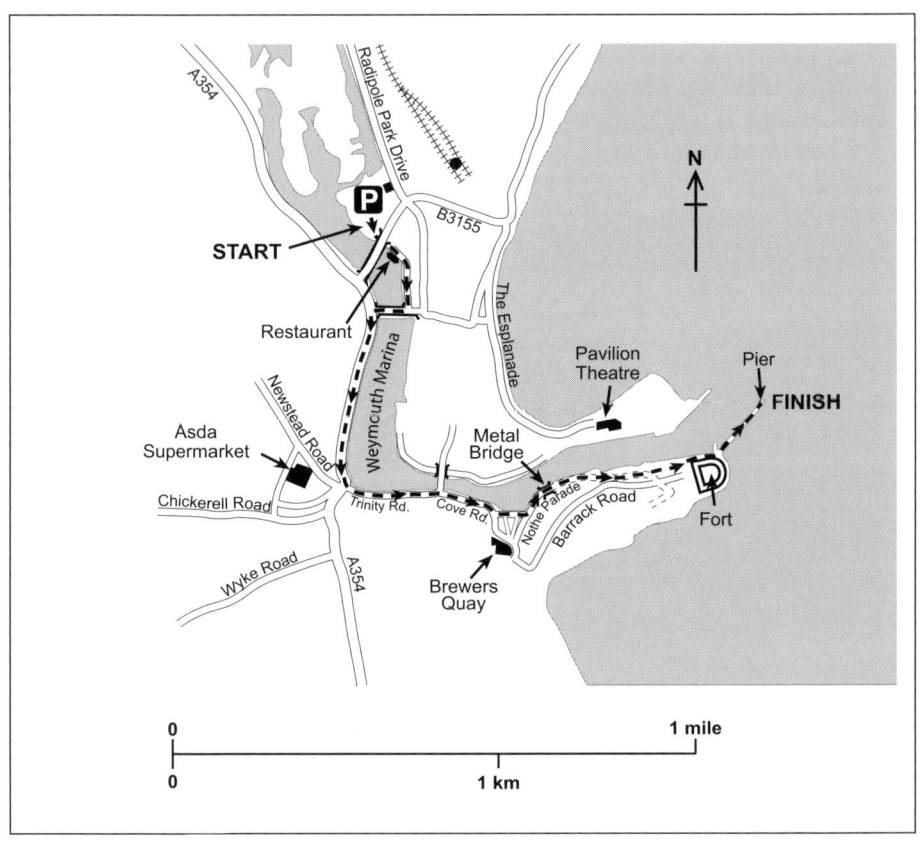

at here. If you take some time to stop and look into the water, you can also see lots of large grey mullets fish swimming close to the harbour walls.

As you follow the path around the harbour, passing a large supermarket on the right, you will come to a bridge that opens up to let boats and yachts through into the marina. This is an interesting thing for children to watch if you time the walk right. Cross over the road and walk and keep following the harbour side.

The harbour will be on your left and houses, cafes and pubs on the right. At the first turning on the right you will be able to see the 'Brewers Quay, which is a converted Victorian brewery.

Keep walking alongside the harbour, with the water to your left and the houses to your right. You will eventually cross over a metal bridge. As you continue on this path you will see a building directly in your path, with a sign on it. If you look to your left you will see the Weymouth Pavilion Theatre directly opposite, across the harbour. When you reach this building, turn immediately right and the path will take you past some steps on the right up to Nothe Gardens and on towards the pier.

You will pass the walls of Nothe Fort on your right, which was built as part of the defence of Portland years ago. As you walk on you will reach the pier and the end of the harbour. There are plenty of stone/concrete seats on the pier and at the end of the pier is a viewing platform. Once you have enjoyed the views across the harbour you will need to retrace your steps.

What to see and do
Explore the many craft shops alongside the old harbour area or take some time out to explore Nothe Fort.
There is a small play park opposite the restaurant based on a boat. You will also find plenty of mallards, swans and other birds to feed here too.

What to look out for
There are hundreds of sea gulls throughout this walk and they are very happy to try their luck at stealing food from you.
Enjoy looking at all of the yachts and boats in the Weymouth Marina and harbour.
Grey mullets can be found in the harbour waters. These are very common here, but apparently very difficult to catch.

WALK 21
The Rodwell Trail

This is a beautiful and tranquil walk along the trail of the old railway line between Weymouth and Ferrybridge. There are amazing views over to

Distance	3.8 miles (6 km)
Parking	There is parking at the Chesil Beach car park, which can be found on the main A354 causeway into Portland. They also have designated disabled parking spaces. The postcode for this whole area is DT4 9BD, ensure you keep going towards Portland and onto the causeway, the car park will be on the right. Charges do apply and it is worth noting that this car park is situated approximately a quarter of a mile from the start of the trail, so please factor this into the time required to complete the walk. There is also the option of parking behind the Ferrybridge public house for a small fee (No designated disabled parking spaces), which is directly opposite the start of the trail and the postcode is DT4 9AF - ensure you drive far enough down the road as again this postcode covers a wide area
Facilities	Pub, café, toilets at the Chesil Beach car park (Accessible toilet available) and Sandsfoot Gardens and Café, benches and bins
Gradient	Flat
Terrain	Tarmac
Map	OS Explorer OL15

Portland and out over the English Channel. It is quite awe inspiring to be able to see Portland Harbour and to imagine the amount of activity that must have taken place here over the last few hundred years, especially when it was used as the main base for the channel.

As the terrain is all tarmac this makes it a delightful walk for everyone.

View over the channel

The Area

The trail was opened for passengers and goods in 1865 and took its last passengers in March 1952. It was used as a passage for freight for a further 13 years, but eventually the line was closed completely in April 1965.

As you complete the walk you will see several of the old platforms. There is also the opportunity to stop for refreshments at Sandsfoot 'Gardens and Ruin', which offers great views and history.

Undisturbed by trains since 1965, this trail has now become a haven for wildlife. This path is very popular with cyclists, dog walkers, history and train enthusiasts, nature lovers and those who simply want to take in the stunning views across the water.

The Walk

The trail starts directly opposite the Ferrybridge public house. With your back to the road and the public house walk on the tarmac path and alongside a small beach area on your right. If you wanted to have a picnic here either before or after the walk, there is a small slope about 50 metres from the road on the right, which allows you to get straight onto the beach.

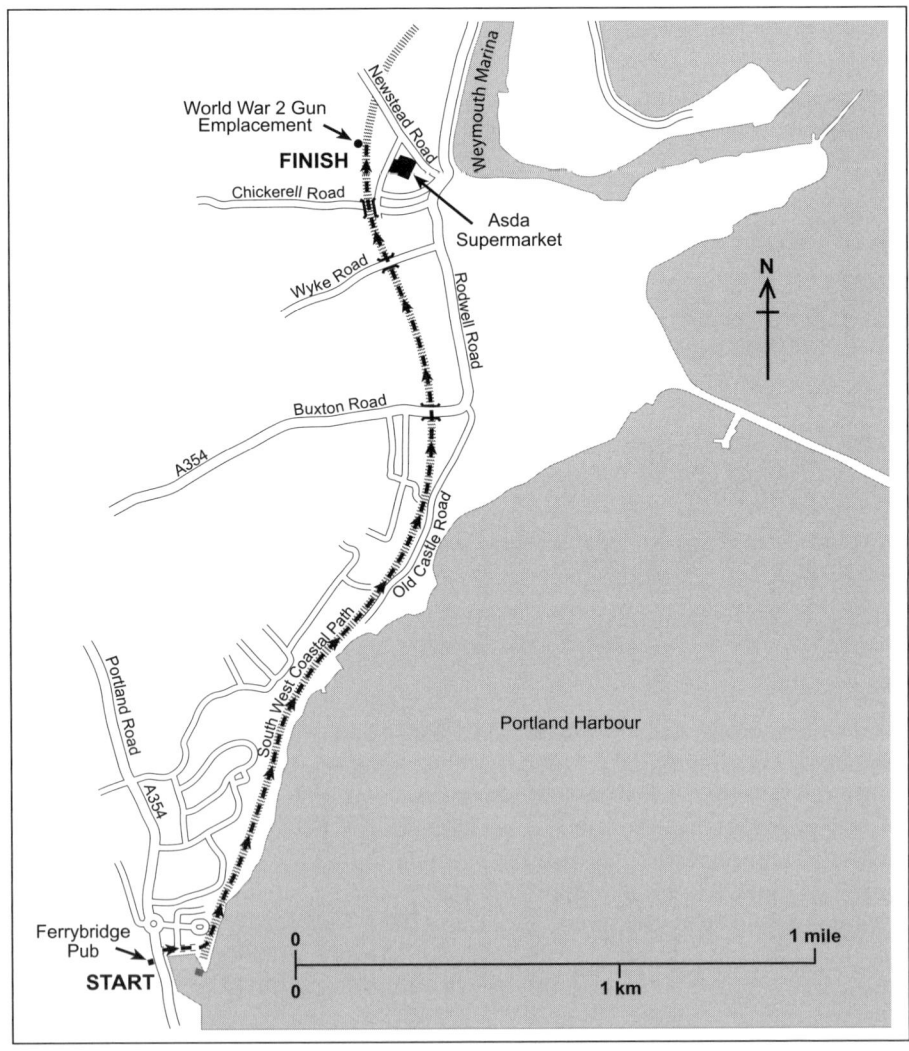

Sandsfoot garden and ruins (FAV)

As you continue on the trail you will have residential houses on your left and the water on your right. There are various tracks that lead off to the left into the residential areas, however you are going to be walking straight on until you reach the end of the trail way.

You will pass through Old Wyke Regis Hall station and platform where you feel like you are walking through the middle of two large banks. This is simply where brambles and other plant life have overgrown on either side of the track. After this the path opens up quite significantly and you can then see the white cliffs of the shoreline across the water.

After 1.45km there is a turning to the right, which is signposted 'Sandsfoot Gardens and Café'. This is a lovely place to get refreshments and to explore the ruins. Parts of the area are wheelchair accessible.

As you continue on this path you will walk under a brick bridge and through a woodland area, which was actually the home of the Rodwell platform and station. It is very peaceful and tranquil here and no doubt in total contrast to the busy station it once was.

Continue on and walk through the brick tunnel and you will now be able to see views of Weymouth Harbour. The end of the trail is the large, seated area on the left, which is actually a refurbished World War 2 Anti-Aircraft gun emplacement. This is the end of the walk and you now need to retrace your steps.

What to see and do
Explore the historical gardens and ruins of Sandsfoot, while enjoying some light refreshments from the café.
   Older children may enjoy riding their bikes on this smooth surface.

What to look out for
There really is an abundance of wildlife on this walk. A huge number of birds can be found here from the larger species such as the Kestral and gull to smaller birds such as the Robin and Blue tit.
   There will be lots of boats and yachts on the water and if you look over to Portland you will be able to see some of the huge carrier ships.

WALK 22
Dorchester River Walk

This is a lovely flat walk alongside the River Frome in Dorchester. It takes in a small nature reserve and some local history, before leading you to the family friendly 'Sun Inn', at the end of this route. This is an ideal place to enjoy some refreshments before following the route back to your car.

Distance	2.2 miles (3.6km)
Parking	You can park along the main High West/East Street in Dorchester or in any of the town car parks (Disabled Parking bays in the town car parks) – charges do apply Monday to Saturday. The walk starts along the B3150 (London Road end) in Dorchester. As you travel down High East Street in Dorchester the road goes over a bridge and then becomes London Road. Immediately after the bridge there is a footpath, which leads to the riverside and this is the start of the walk
Facilities	Benches, bins, dog bins and pub (The Sun Inn has disabled access). There are more cafes, restaurants and toilet facilities in the town centre. There is an accessible toilet in Antelope Walk that requires a RADAR key; this is opposite the tourist information centre in the town centre and approximately 100 metres from the start of the walk
Gradient	The majority of the route is flat – the only exceptions are one small hump in the nature reserve and then the hump back bridges, which have a slight incline and decline, however they are all very minimal

Terrain	Tarmac, several wooden bridges, mesh covered boardwalk through the nature reserve and one short section of woodland, i.e. mud, leaves etc
Map	OS Explorer OL15

The Area

Dorchester is a lovely town with some fascinating history. Interestingly Thomas Hardy set one of his novels 'The Mayor of Casterbridge' in Dorchester. His home 'Max Gate' is situated on the outskirts of Dorchester and is now owned and maintained by the National Trust.

The small nature reserve can be found in a very natural state, the only work that appears to have been done here is the laying of the wooded boardwalk. You are seeing nature in its purest form!

This is a popular walk for dog walkers and bird enthusiasts.

The Walk

As you stand by the bridge on London Road, you will see a black metal open kissing gate, which is wide enough for a double pushchair. Go through this and you will now be walking alongside the River Frome. There are no barriers between the pathway and the stream at the start of the walk, so please take care with children and dogs. The water is not very deep but wet children or dogs could spoil your walk!

Keep on this main walkway until you come across a turning to your right, which is the start of the boardwalk through the small nature reserve. There is only one short section of approximately 20 metres at the end of the reserve, where the wooded boardwalk changes to a woodland terrain before rejoining the main path alongside the river. It may be best to avoid this short section if you are in a wheelchair.

When you rejoin the main path you need to turn right and continue alongside the river. You will have allotments on your right and houses on the left. Soon there will be a small rest area with an information board and a picnic table; from here you will have fields, woodland and meadows on the right.

At the end of this path you will come to a T Junction with a path that leads into the town centre to the left and a path to the right which goes over a wooden bridge. You will also notice a pond to your right called John's Pond,

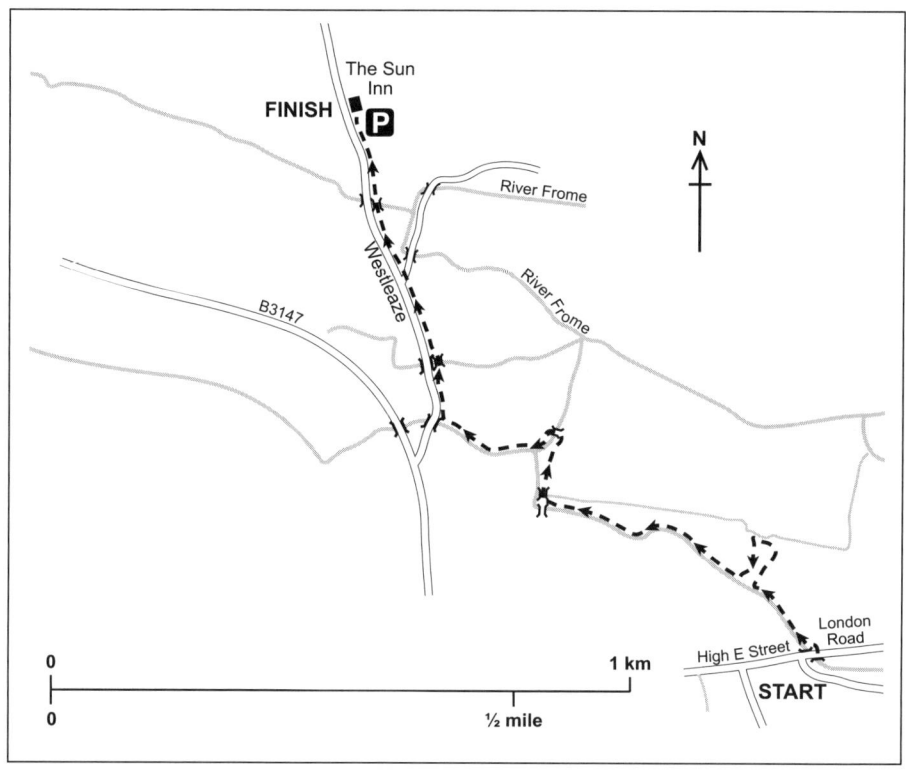

legend has it that a prisoner called John drowned in this pond after escaping from the local gaol. If you look straight ahead you will see a cottage that used to be home to the town executioner.

Take the path to the right and go over the wooden bridge, the river will now be on your left and you will have beautiful fields to your right, if you are very lucky you may catch sight of a buzzard. This seems to be a popular place to bird spot with locals and you will often see people with binoculars looking out across the fields and towards the woodland.

You will then come to another bridge on your left, which you need to cross over. There will be a sign on the bridge saying 'Sun Inn'. As you walk down this path the river will still be on your left. The path will shortly take you by the main road and in front of you and slightly to the left you will be able to see the signs of the petrol station on the outskirts of Dorchester.

River Frome

Follow the path around to the right, which is sign posted to 'Charminster' and you will need to walk over another wooden bridge. You will now have the road on your left and the fields on your right. To your left you will pass a brown tourist sign poking out over the hedgerows saying 'Sun Inn – 350 yards'. When you reach the private lane, cross straight over and walk towards and over the last wooden bridge. The Sun Inn will be directly in front of you. This is the end of your walk and when you are ready you can turn around and head back to the start of the walk.

What to see and do
There is a vast amount of history in Dorchester which locals are very proud of. You could take the time to read more about their literary connections or even visit one of their many interesting museums, such as the Dinosaur and Tutankhamen museums.

What to look out for
There were plenty of hungry ducks swimming in the river. The fields were full of crows looking for food and we walked by just as a large buzzard flew into sight.

WALK 23
Cannon Hill

This is a lovely circular walk around Cannon Hill, following one of the main tracks through Ferndown Forest. The paths throughout the walk are lovely and wide, although can get wet and muddy depending on the weather. There are a couple of ascents that require effort, but nothing too strenuous as long as you are fit and prepared for a bit of extra effort. This is best completed with an all-terrain pushchair.

I would not recommend this walk for those in a wheelchair.

Distance	2 miles (3.18km)
Parking	There is a free car park at the start of the trail. As you travel from towards Ringwood on the A31 you will go straight over a roundabout that has two junctions entering onto it from the B3073, this is situated just after Wimborne Minster. Shortly after this roundabout you will see a road on the left signposted 'Holt, Broom Hill and Garden Centre', this is Uddens Drive. Approximately 50 meters from the junction and on the left you will see the green and white forestry commission sign for the forest and you can park here
Facilities	A couple of benches, café at the Garden Centre in Broom Hill another mile on. The Fox and Hounds public house just off of the B3073 in Fox Lane, this is the second exit of the first roundabout you come to as you head back towards Dorchester from Uddens Road on the A31
Gradient	The walk does undulate in places, with one long ascent – the good news is that once you reach the top the rest of the walk is all downhill!

Terrain	Gravel and woodland, which can get muddy at certain times of the year
Map	OS Explorer OL22

The Area
The whole of Ferndown Forest is very popular with outdoor enthusiasts as it allows for a number of activities, i.e. walking, cycling and horse riding. You will also see a number of dog owners exercising their pets. There are plenty of interesting things to explore and sniff and big puddles to splash around in!

The Walk
From the car park you will see a green metal gate in front of you, go around this and you will then find yourself on a wide gravel path. You will be staying on this main path throughout the walk and ignoring any paths that lead off to the left and the right.

As you walk to the end of this first section you will see that the main path bends around to the right, follow this track and continue on. You will pass

Path at Cannon Hill

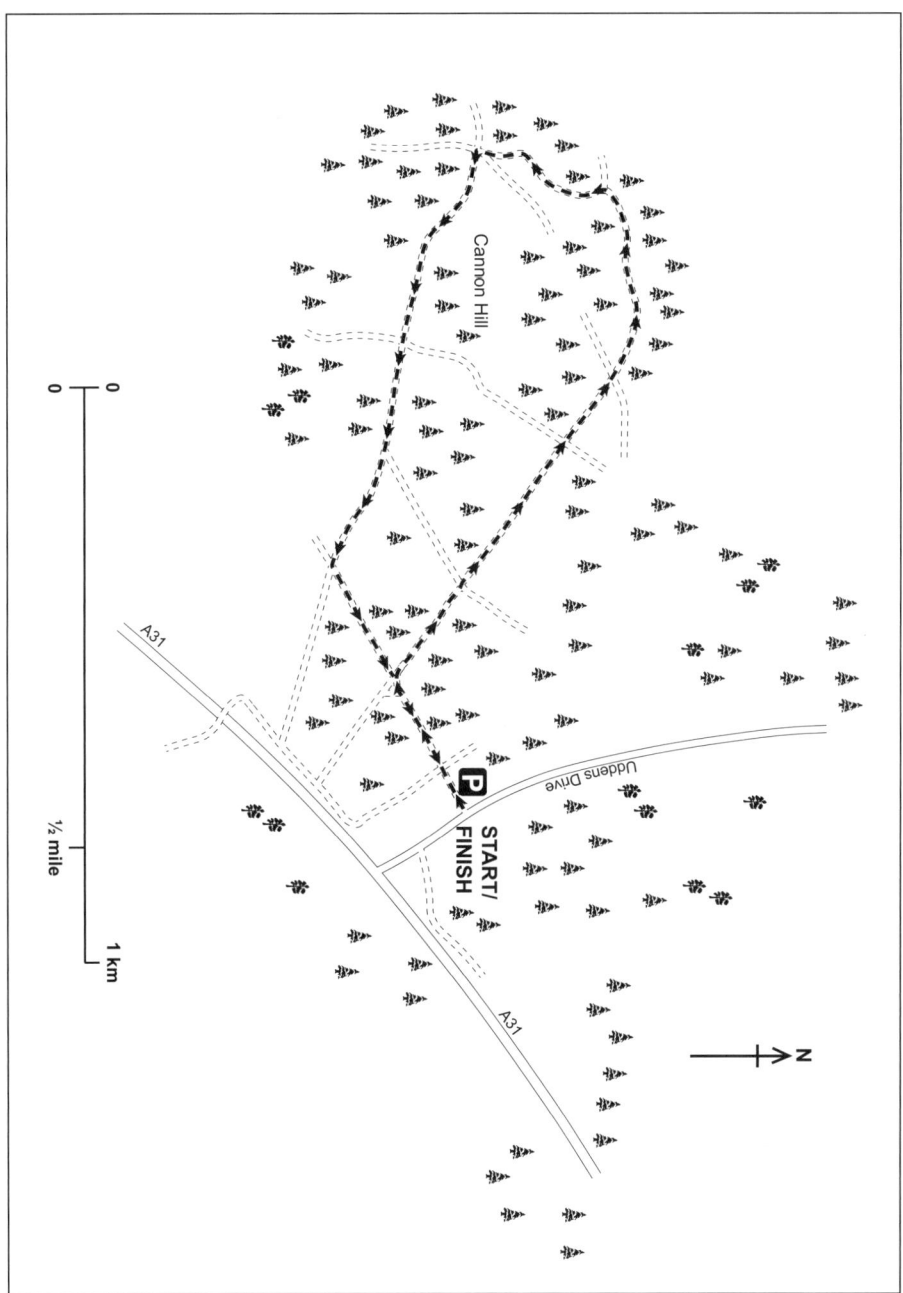

several tracks along this section of the walk that lead into the wood, however they are not all accessible and so I would not advise exploring unless you don't mind retracing your steps.

You will come to a section in the walk where the track bends to the left and then starts a gentle ascent. When you are about half way up this ascent, you will see a track that takes you off to the right, however you need to stay on the main track that continues on up the hill. Although the climb is not particularly steep it does cover approximately 400 metres, so I was a little out of puff by the time I reached the top. The views back over the forest were lovely though and certainly worth the effort.

As you walk on, you will come to some crossroads and you need to continue straight on. If you look to your right you will see a house behind a wooden fence. At the next crossroads, you will be taking the path to the left. If you look to the right this time you will see a clearly defined path that leads in front of a fence and a white house, this is the start of the residential area.

This part of the track can get a little muddy when it has been raining, so wellingtons are advised. Our daughter loved splashing in the puddles and getting covered in mud!

At the next crossroads go straight over and you will come to the old burial area. If you take the path to the left this will take you around the burial mound and there is a bench and a lovely viewpoint over the forest. The path to the right of the burial ground is the one that will take you on a descent and back towards the car park. The path is a little steep and bumpy in places due to tree roots, however once again the all-terrain pushchair made light work of it.

When you get to the bottom of the hill you will see a signpost with two blue signs on it, one pointing ahead and the other to the right. You will be walking straight ahead on the wider and more obvious path and past the two paths on the right and the path on the left, which is an alternative route down from the burial mound.

When you get to the next crossroads, walk straight ahead and in the far distance you will be able to see the car park. This section of the trail comes out on the main track that you started on, simply walk straight ahead and back down the track to the car park.

What to see and do
Older children could practice their mountain biking skills on the wide paths – the muddy patches may be slightly more challenging for very young riders. It is also a great place for children to explore as the paths are wide and long, which allow you to keep youngsters in sight.

You could enjoy some refreshments at the local garden centre or even at the Fox and Hounds public house.

What to look out for
There is a burial ground on the walk, which caused our dog to get spooked!

A variety of trees and wildlife can be spotted here. There were plenty of pine and fir trees and the occasional holly bush with hundreds of vibrant red berries growing on it.

This is definitely a popular destination for horse lovers and as such we met several horse riders trekking through the forest.

WALK 24
Milldown Nature Reserve

This is a delightful little walk around the perimeter of the local nature reserve, found on the north side of Blandford. It is very popular with families and dog owners and as such is a hugely social walk. Although the walk around the reserve is less than one mile, you can extend it by an additional mile if you wish to take in the old Somerset and Dorset Trailway and walk down into Blandford town centre.

Distance	0.9miles (1.52km)
Parking	As you travel through Blandford on the B3082 and head towards the A350, you will be on Milldown Road. There will be the Blandford Community Hospital on your right and a primary school on your left. Shortly after the school, you will see the green signs on the right for the nature reserve. The postcode for this area is DT11 7SN. There is parking in designated spaces before and after the railway bridge and no charges apply. There are no disabled parking spaces, but you should have no trouble parking
Facilities	Benches, picnic benches, bins and dog bins. There are cafes and pubs within Blandford town centre. Public toilets can be found in West Street, next to the Tourist Information Centre
Gradient	Predominately flat, with one short gentle incline
Terrain	Tarmac
Map	OS Explorer OL118

The Area
The reserve has been listed as a 'Site of Nature Conservation Interest', which means that it adds value in some way to the local area. With the abundance of flora and fauna that can be found on its 38.5 acres, it is very easy to see why.

The Walk
Head towards the tarmac path on the left side of the large green area, this is situated in front of the car park. You will see a notice board on the left side of the path, this is the start of the walk and you will be walking clockwise around the perimeter of the nature reserve.

As you walk around the first part of the route you will have fields, woodland and open meadows to your left. There is a huge log on the grass that appears to be a permanent fixture, which my daughter took great delight in climbing on.

As you get half way around you will have a slight incline and the scenery to the left changes. You will now be walking alongside the back of residential areas. This part of the path will take you on a gentle slope back down to the car park.

Milldown nature reserve

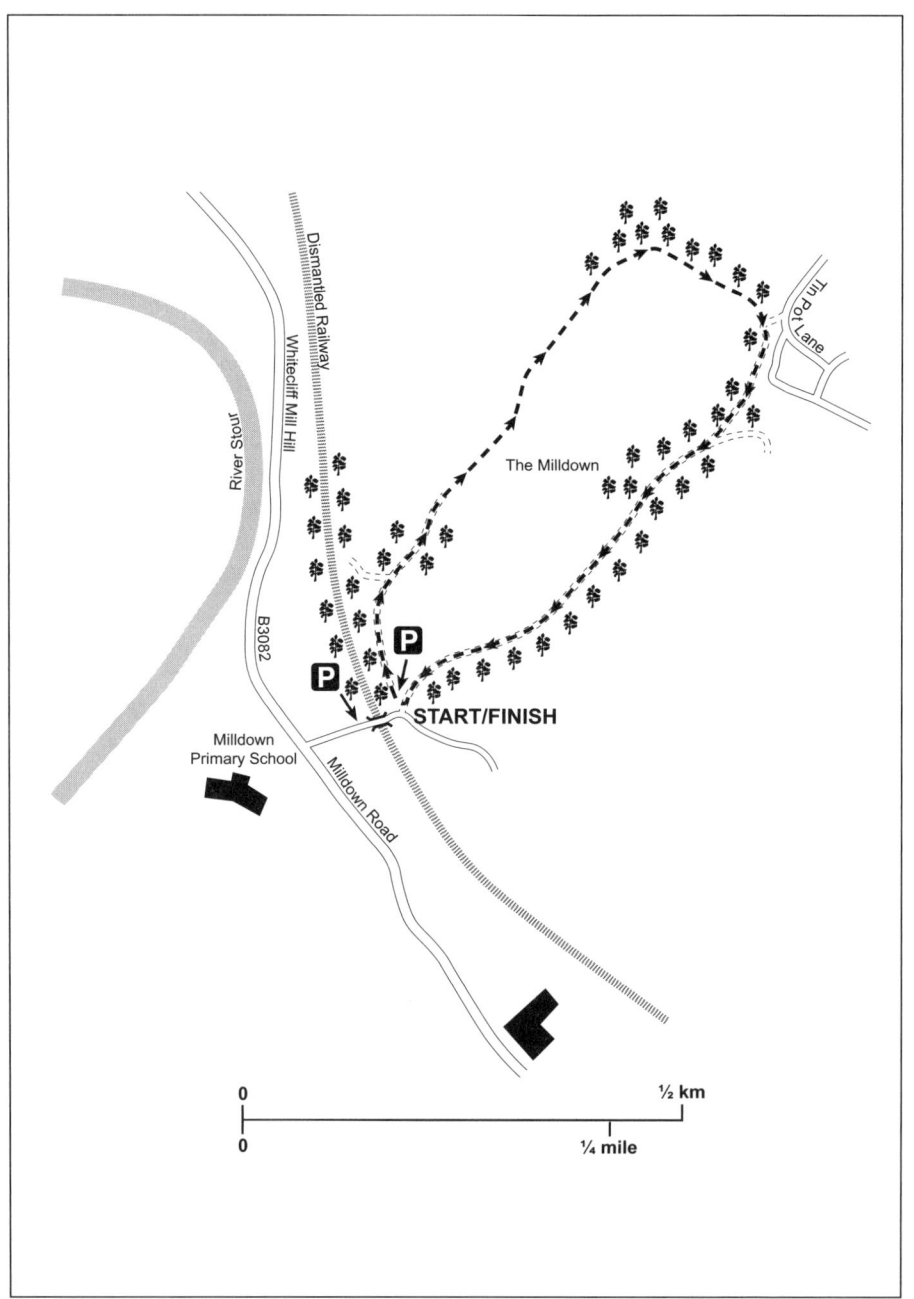

What to see and do
Younger children could cycle or scoot around the tarmac path. Many families were playing games of football on the green.

What to look out for
The woodland and grassland areas are home to a variety of butterflies and moths. It is believed that over 60 different types of bird visit the reserve and over 200 different varieties of wild flower grow here.

We were able to spot crows in the neighbouring field and a couple of squirrels. There were definitely other birds singing in the trees, although we were not able to identify them.

WALK 25
North Dorset Trailway – Shillingston to Stourpaine

This is a lovely linear walk along the old Somerset and North Dorset railway line. It meanders through the Dorset countryside and past some very quaint and traditional villages. It is a peaceful walk with far reaching views across fields and meadows. Taking in various sections of the River Stour you will catch sight of some fantastic wildlife and the view of the river from the newly built railway bridge is truly wonderful.

The walk is predominately flat, apart from one short steep section that requires a bit more effort. The all-terrain pushchair had no trouble with this at all. If you were in a wheelchair you could simply choose to turn around at this point.

Distance	6 miles (9.6km)
Parking	As you travel from Blandford on the A357 you will go through the village of Shillingstone. As you leave the village you will see a turning on the right for Child Okeford. This one way road is called Bere Marsh and shortly turns into Haywards Lane. The start of the walk is just after the railway bridge on the right. The postcode for the area is DT11 0QY. There is parking for 3 cars by the railway bridge, with the unofficial overflow being the right side of Bere Marsh road, leading up to the junction of the A357. There are no designated disabled spaces
Facilities	Benches, bins, dog bins, play park, toilets at Shillingstone Station however there is restricted access and opening hours (only open on a Wednesday, Saturday and Sunday 10am-4pm), café at the Shillingstone Station (again only open on a Wednesday,

Facilities (cont'd)	Saturday and Sunday 10am-4pm), pub at Stourpaine (this is an extra ¼ miles from the end of the trail)
Gradient	Mainly flat, there are a couple of gentle inclines and declines and one short steep section of about 40 metres
Terrain	Predominately gravel, tarmac and a couple of short concrete sections. There were a couple of short sections that were muddy
Map	OS Explorer OL118

The Area

Shillingstone is a village based in the north of Dorset between Blandford and Sturminster Newton.

This walk is hugely popular with ramblers, dog owners and cyclists, especially as it is part of a national Cycle Route. The Trailway is also a bridleway and you may see horse and riders along the way.

The path could get muddy in places if there has been a lot of rain, so wellingtons might be a good choice for children.

The Walk

You will be staying on the main path all the way to Stourpaine and ignoring any paths that veer off to the left and right. You will go over several bridges including the newly built Stourpaine railway bridge, which allows fantastic views of the river.

With your back to the bridge, take the Trailway path on the right. There is a gentle slope here taking you up to the path that leads to the Shillingstone Railway Project. You will have residential homes to your right and open fields and meadows to your left.

When you arrive at the Shillingstone Railway Project, you will walk past the railway station by using the old platform. As you look across the track you will see the restored station buildings, including a quaint little museum and tearoom.

As you continue on you will soon come to a bird hide on the left, which looks directly down towards the river. This is an ideal place to see the river wildlife up close, in particular birds looking for food in and near the river.

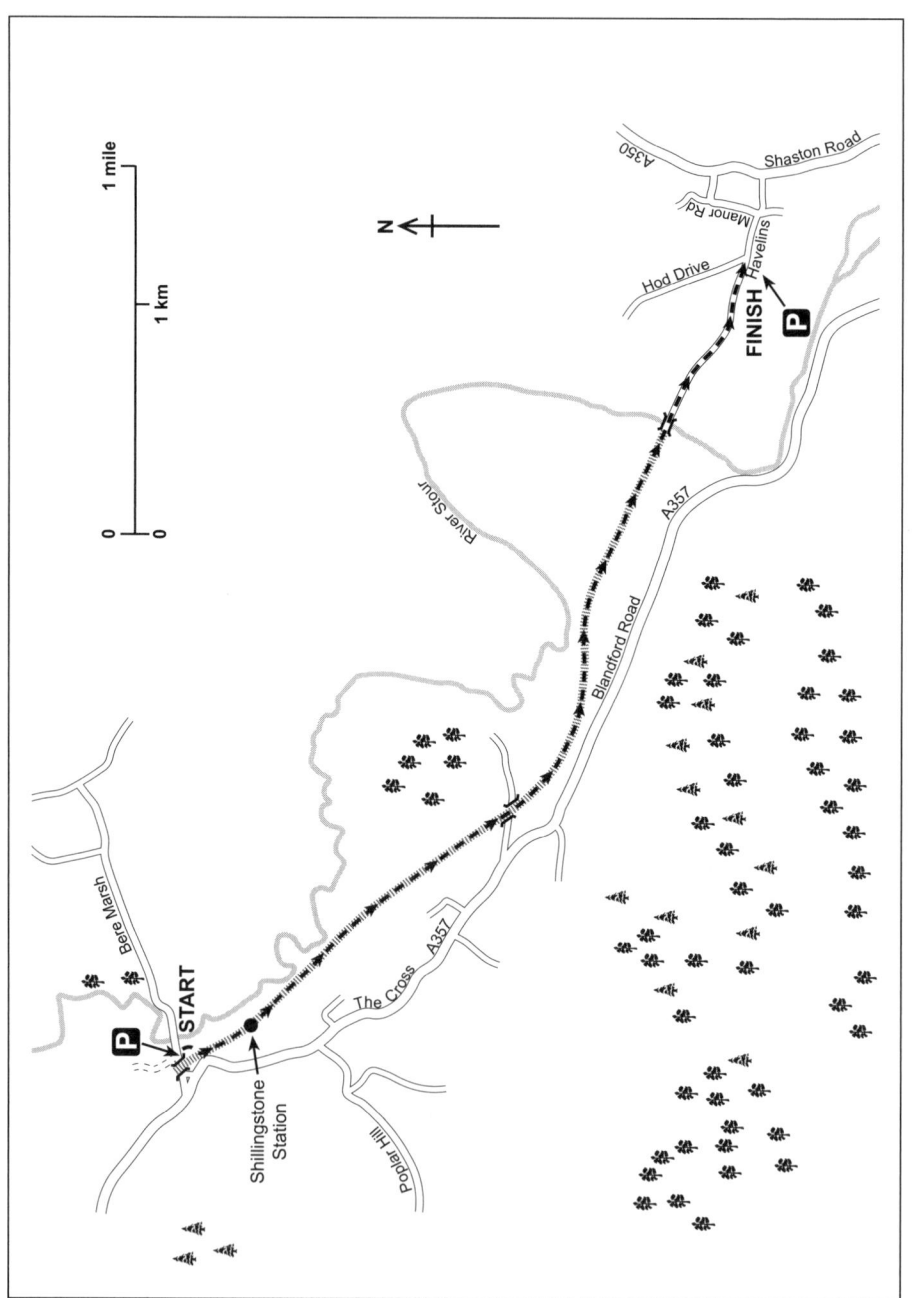

Shortly after the bird hide you will see playing fields to your right, with a little children's play ground should you wish to let children play. A metal gate directly opposite a wooden sign to 'Old Ox Inn' will give you access to the recreational area.

After approximately 1.5 miles, you will reach a steep hill that leads onto a track that resembles a quiet country lane. Don't be put off by the hill as it really is easy enough with an all-terrain pushchair and the climb is only for a short distance. At the end of this section of the track you will come to a cross roads, with a farm track directly to your left and a track that is sign posted to 'Blandford Forest' on your right. You will see that the Trailway continues straight on after slightly staggering to the left for a couple of meters.

This finely gritted path takes you on a long and gentle slope downhill before taking you over the newly built bridge. You will then walk through a wooded and hedged area, before arriving at the edge of Stourpaine village and the end of this section of the Trailway. You will see playing fields and a private car park on your right and a sign directing you straight ahead for the local public house, which is situated a quarter of a mile away. You have now reached the end of the walk and when you are ready turn around and start the journey back to Shillingstone.

What to see and do
There is the Shillingstone Railway Project at the start of the walk, which is a great historical place to explore. It is the last surviving station built by the Dorset Central Railway and hence much work is undertaken here by dedicated people, keen to ensure its preservation. They do have restricted opening hours as mentioned above, so it would be best to double check opening hours before setting out, particularly if you wanted to combine your walk with a visit here.

The Trailway is a great place for older and more independent children to cycle if they do not want to walk.

There are children's play parks near the beginning of the walk in Shillingstone and at Stourpaine.

What to look out for
As the walk takes you through the heart of the countryside you will see a variety of farmyard animals, such as sheep, cows and horses.

At the start of the walk and on your left, you will often see lots of fisherman on the banks of the River Stour. This is a very popular location for catching pike, roach and perch.

Shillingstone station

There are plenty of birds here and we were lucky enough to see a buzzard hovering over the fields looking for a tasty snack from the field below.

Also from Sigma Leisure:

South West England Nature Walks
from train stations
Graeme Down

Get away from it all and find nature using the train! Although the countryside is easily accessible by car, it's far more relaxing to combine the beauty of the countryside with the less stressful mode of train travel. Twenty-four circular walks are described, starting and finishing at stations across the south-west, keeping off road as much as possible, and taking the walker through landscapes from fens to farmland and coastal surf to chalk downland. There are two walks for each month of the year, timed to give maximum chance of spotting the wildlife on offer. Each route is clearly described and accompanied by a map. Along the way, hints are given to help the reader identify some of the wildlife they may be able to find.
£8.99

Family Walks in Hampshire
in and around The Meon Valley
Louis Murray

The river Meon is one of Hampshire's quintessential chalk streams. It rises from natural springs in the South Downs to the south of the village of East Meon. This book contains the details of 20 walks in the Meon river valley area in southern Hampshire. The walks are suitable for novices, casual walkers, family groups, and experienced ramblers.
£8.99

Discover Cornwall
20 walks to explore the county
Sue Kittow

Cornwall's fine golden sands have provided the backdrop for many childhood holidays, but it is also a wonderful county to explore on foot. As well as the coastal footpath, there are numerous less known routes that are great fun to investigate. There are a good range of gentle to moderate walks between 4 and 6 miles in length. Discover Cornwall lists 20 walks providing a healthy and entertaining way to keep fit, learn about Cornwall, and enjoy the beaches, moorland and hisotry of this magical county. The walks have clear directions, delightful details and excellent photographs, maing this a unique book to keep and pore over for readers as well as walkers.
£8.99

Cornwall Walking on the level
Norman & June Buckley

This book selects and illustrates 28 routes, mainly circular, which explore some of the finest parts of the county, without serious ascent. In addition to the route directions, the distance, ascent, car parking, refreshment and map, with a succinct assessment, are provided for each walk.
£8.99

All of our books are all available on-line at **www.sigmapress.co.uk** or through booksellers. For a free catalogue, please contact:

Sigma Leisure, Stobart House, Pontyclerc, Penybanc Road, Ammanford, Carmarthenshire SA18 3HP
Tel: 01269 593100   Fax: 01269 596116
info@sigmapress.co.uk   www.sigmapress.co.uk